The
Old Testament Roots
of Our Faith

PAUL J. and ELIZABETH ACHTEMEIER

The
Old Testament Roots
of Our Faith

FORTRESS PRESS   PHILADELPHIA

Scripture quotations unless otherwise noted are from the Revised Standard Version of the Bible, copyright 1946 and 1952 by the Division of Christian Education of the National Council of the Churches of Christ in the U.S.A., and are used by permission.

First Fortress Press edition 1979

Library of Congress Cataloging in Publication Data

Achtemeier, Paul J
  The Old Testament roots of our faith.

  Reprint of the ed. published by Abingdon Press, New York.
  Bibliography: p.
  Includes index.
  1. God—Promises—Biblical teaching. 2. Bible. O. T.—Theology. I. Achtemeier, Elizabeth Rice, 1926- joint author. II. Title.
  [BS1192.6.A25 1979]   230'.09   78-14659
  ISBN 0-8006-1348-1

7395I78   Printed in the United States of America   1-1348

In Gratitude
to Our Parents

PREFACE

We welcome the reissuance of this book. Over the years we have learned many new things which we would happily have included in this republication. There was however no opportunity for extensive revisions. Our world also has changed, and, with it, linguistic conventions. Feminists will surely be disturbed at our generic use of the term "man" throughout the book. The economics of current publishing precluded any textual changes other than some corrections of typographical errors. We believe the book still provides the lay reader a basic understanding of the Old Testament witness to what God has done for our salvation, and in that faith we have allowed its republication.

Paul J. and Elizabeth Achtemeier

Contents

9

Why Bother with the Old Testament?

Perhaps no book seems more remote and less necessary to life in the twentieth century than does the Old Testament. To most of us the volume is, as its title suggests, very old. In fact, it seems antiquated—a musty, dusty collection of ancient writings which have little relevance to our modern life and no interest for the space-age man.

We are therefore not too concerned with our ignorance of the Old Testament. We know a little about it. We can quote a few of its more familiar passages or at least the twenty-third Psalm. We remember from our childhood days its stories about Joseph and David and Daniel. We recognize its great lyrical passages when we hear them read and sung: "For unto us a child is born . . ." or perhaps "Lift up your heads, O ye gates!" (KJV). But this knowledge seems entirely adequate in our present faith, and to go beyond it would appear largely a waste of time.

The truth of the matter is that to those of us who really want to be Christians, the Old Testament seems outdated by the New. Its view that God acts in jealousy and wrath seems antiquated by the higher Christian concept of the love of a heavenly Father. Its law appears to be a burden unnecessary to a religion which knows justification by faith alone. Its view of Israel as the chosen people seems the outgrowth of a repugnant national pride which has led to nothing but the persecution of the Jews. The Old Testament religion, in the thought of most of us, has been replaced by one far superior.

When we add to this our view of the nature of the Old Testament writings, we become convinced we should not bother with the volume. We read its stories and find in them moral lessons which, however necessary to children in Sunday school, cannot match the insights of modern psychology. The history in the book seems dry as dust and of interest only to the scholars. And all of this is surrounded by a thousand begats, the jaw-breaking names of innumerable kings, and unbelievable miracle tales. It is little wonder that laymen give lip service to the Old Testament as part of our Bible, but ignore it as much as possible. It does not seem like the kind of book with which we either need or want to bother.

And yet, for those of us who truly want to be Christian, for those among us who desire to grow and mature in the faith, the Old Testament is an absolutely indispensable volume. It is indispensable because we must enter into a living and personal relationship with Jesus Christ. And without the Old Testament we do not know fully who Jesus Christ is.

Our Lord once asked his disciples, "Who do men say that I am?" Their reply was, "John the Baptist; and others say, Elijah; and others, one of the prophets." (Mark 8:27-29.) But then Jesus asked the crucial question: "Who do you say that I am?" The disciples were confronted squarely with the basic decision of the Christian faith.

Who is Jesus Christ? Upon our answer to this question hang all of our lives and hopes. If Jesus of Nazareth was a man who lived long ago; if, in our decision, he was a great moral teacher and an exemplary saint, then he may serve as a limited pattern for our lives, and we may be grateful for his example. But ultimately, he has nothing of lasting value to give to the twentieth century. History has passed him by. He lived in an age when a man's problems were limited to the regions of the Mediterranean. And he died with the assurance that the majority of the human race would continue in existence after him. We face world-wide perplexities and threats of annihilation with which he was never forced to cope. Many of his answers to problems are no longer relevant to our age.

But if Jesus of Nazareth was more than a moral man, if he was indeed the Messiah of God, as Peter confessed at Caesarea Philippi; if he was God completing a promise and directing history to a goal; if he was faithfulness triumphant over rebellion, and mercy defeating hate; if he was a victorious Lord astride the beast of history, then he is in truth the most important fact in the twentieth century. He is God holding fast to a world which is shaking and writhing to loose the divine grasp. He is the guarantee that the power of that grasp neither weakens nor tires. He is in truth the hand of God holding up the universe while shaping with a couple of fingers our planet into the form of a Kingdom.

All of these affirmations about Jesus Christ do not rest solely upon the witness of the New Testament, however. They rest upon the witness of both the New and the Old. For the New Testament itself constantly refers us to the Old Testament in order to tell us who Jesus is.

This is true of the very first sentence in the New Testament. At the beginning of the Gospel According to Matthew, we read, "The book of the genealogy of Jesus Christ, the son of

David, the son of Abraham." Immediately we are back in the Old Testament, for the very first thing that Matthew can think to tell us about our Lord is that he is of Hebrew descent. And so to know who Jesus Christ is, we must know something about the Hebrew David and Abraham.

The same seems true throughout the New Testament. When we read Stephen's defense or Paul's sermon at Antioch in the Book of Acts (7; 13:16-41), we expect to find some of the church's earliest descriptions of Jesus of Nazareth. And yet they start not with Jesus or with the cross, but with the men of the Old Testament—Abraham, Joseph, Moses, Samuel, Saul, and David. And throughout the Gospel records, we are sent back to the Old Testament's history. Consider just three verses of the many from Luke and John:

> Philip found Nathanael, and said to him, "We have found him of whom Moses in the law and also the prophets wrote, Jesus of Nazareth, the son of Joseph." (John 1:45.)
> And taking the twelve, he said to them, "Behold, we are going up to Jerusalem, and everything that is written of the Son of man by the prophets will be accomplished." (Luke 18:31.)
> And [Jesus] said to them, "O foolish men, and slow of heart to believe all that the prophets have spoken! Was it not necessary that the Christ should suffer these things and enter into his glory?" And beginning with Moses and all the prophets, he interpreted to them in all the scriptures the things concerning himself. (Luke 24:25-27.)

Jesus Christ is, in the thought of the New Testament, the culmination and completion of an action of God which began not on that first Christmas night in Bethlehem of Judaea, but somewhere around 1750 B.C. in Mesopotamia with the first patriarch of the Hebrew people. Or to put it in another way, Christianity did not start with the events recorded in the New Testament. It started with the events recorded in the twelfth chapter of Genesis. It started when God said to Abraham, "Go from your country and your kindred and your father's house to the land that I will show you."

If, then, we are to understand this faith of ours, if we are to know Jesus Christ as the New Testament knows him, if we are to comprehend his actions as Paul or Stephen or the disciples comprehended them, we, too, must start with their beginning. We must start with the Old Testament story, seeing not only God's final act in Jesus Christ, but also all of his acts before that. The action in Jesus Christ is the summation, the completion, the fulfillment of many events before it. And unless we comprehend that which has gone before, we cannot grasp the full significance and meaning of the end. God has acted out a fearful and wonderful drama in our world, but as with any play, if we do not enter into acts one and two, we will not understand act three.

Moreover, without an understanding of the events of the Old Testament, we cannot fully grasp the essential characteristics of our own religious lives. Paul tells us in the epistle to the Romans that Abraham is the father of us all, the father of every Christian. And in chapter eleven, he explains that the Israel of the Old Testament is the root of a tree into which we have only been grafted as wild branches. That is, the nature of the Christian Church is defined in large measure by the nature of Israel in the Old Testament. What Israel was, or was supposed to be, the Christian Church is. And what God did for Israel is the family background and inheritance of every Christian.

15

We cannot therefore fully understand the nature of our lives as Christians unless we understand the nature of Israel. What did it mean to be the chosen people of God? What was the promise given to Israel and what was his mission in the world? What was his relationship to his Lord and what were his obligations? What was the cost of his discipleship and what was its outcome? All of these questions have a direct bearing upon the life of the Christian Church, because all of them are definitive of our life with our Lord. And yet, none of them can be answered unless we understand the Old Testament. It is only when we grasp its message and enter into its events that we will fully understand who we are as the children of Abraham.

To put it in other words, the Christian Church is, in the understanding of the Bible, the new Israel in Christ. Through faith in our Lord, we inherit the nature and life of the chosen people of the old covenant. In Christ, we become the new Israel, the people of the new covenant. But to know who we are, we must inquire diligently who Israel was in the beginning. What he was to be, we have become through our Lord. In Israel lie the character and meaning of our spiritual existence.

So we must bother with the Old Testament in the twentieth century, if we would be Christians. Across its pages is written the nature of our existence as a church. Within its history is recorded a struggle which God finally won in his Son. Through its people is proclaimed a promise which found fulfillment in the Cross and Resurrection. The roots of our Christian faith lie deep in the Old Testament. We shall learn more fully who Jesus Christ is and who we are, only when we place together with our understanding of the New Testament a grasp and knowledge of the Old.

16

Chapter I

God's Promise: The Beginning of the Biblical History

At one time or another, all of us have heard the phrase, "the twelve tribes of Israel," and we take it to refer to the Hebrew people of the Old Testament. Actually, however, the Hebrew nation, with its twelve-tribed structure, did not come into being until the last part of the thirteenth century B.C. or the first part of the twelfth—dates well along in the Old Testament history and the time when the Hebrews became a settled people in the land of Palestine.

Even then, this so-called nation scarcely deserved the name. It was a mixed lot, made up of separate clans, and portions of various Semitic tribes of mixed blood and with widely differing backgrounds and experiences. Some of its members had forebears who had sojourned in Egypt and come under the Egyptian slave yoke. Others were descendants of groups who had gradually infiltrated into Canaan peacefully over a span of three hundred years. A number were children of those seminomads who had always wandered the edges of civilization in Canaan, seeking seasonal pasture for their flocks. But all came to be banded together in the unique nation called Israel.

There were two elements which held this variegated group together during the twelfth and eleventh centuries B.C. First of all, after their settlement in Palestine, they had a common worship. They were, in technical terms, an amphictyony. This means that they worshiped the same God, Yahweh, which is the name of the Lord in the Old Testament. They had a common shrine, at first located near Shechem and later at Shiloh. And they met together at this shrine at stated intervals, probably every seven years, to renew their allegiance to Yahweh, to worship before his throne, which was the ark, and to hear once more his commandments for their daily lives. Upon renewing their allegiance to the Lord and confirming their willingness to walk according to his will, they then returned to their homes, to pursue their separate occupations, to follow their own customs, and to carry on their political lives in their traditional manners. They were, in short, very disparate and independent folk, united primarily by their allegiance to the same God.

But there was another element which tied the Israelites together. This was their common memory. When they became worshipers of Yahweh and pledged themselves to follow him alone, as members of his people, each new group which joined the amphictyony heard the stories of what Yahweh had done in the past. These stories were not all the same. Some concerned God's miraculous deliverance of a group from Egypt. Others told of wonderful feats of guidance and provision in the desert. A number concerned Yahweh's revelation of himself at a holy mountain. Some were tales of special appearances and blessings on behalf of individuals.

Whatever the nature of the story told and from whichever time or tribe it came, the members of the Israelite amphictyony appropriated these stories as their own, as part of their common memory. Because the tales concerned the same God whom they worshiped, the events in them were not acts which Yahweh had done long ago for some other group. They were events which he had done for all of Israel, for the Israelite amphictyony. The Hebrews considered that it had not been just a few of their forebears who had gone down into Egypt. All of them had fallen victim to the Pharaoh "who knew not Joseph." All of the twelve tribes had been delivered by God. All had been present at Sinai and in the wilderness wanderings. All had crossed the Jordan and conquered the promised land behind Yahweh, "the man of war." That which God had done for a few he had done for the nation, just as today we consider the events of the American revolution to be events wrought on behalf of all citizens of the United States. We were there, being freed from the British yoke. And all of Israel was there, being freed from Egyptian slavery. Israel lived together as a united people on the strength of its common memory, its common participation in the events God had wrought in the past.

Among the many acts of God which Israel remembered was a promise given to a clan chieftain named Abraham. Abraham was an Amorite, a northwest-Semitic seminomad, a peaceful herdsman who came originally from the upper part of Mesopotamia. Probably sometime during the eighteenth century B.C., Abraham left his home in Mesopotamia along with many other Amorites and joined in a migration which spread throughout Syria and Palestine.

But in its traditions about Abraham, Israel remembered that he left his home for a special reason. He left it because God commanded him to leave and because God made him a promise. Here is the way it is put in the Old Testament:

Now the Lord said to Abram, "Go from your country and your kindred and your father's house to the land that I will show you. And I will make of you a great nation, and I will bless you, and make your name great, so that you will be a blessing. I will bless those who bless you, and him who curses you I will curse; and by you all the families of the earth will bless themselves." (Gen. 12:1-3.)

Abraham was part of a historical migration of Semitic peoples into Palestine, but the Hebrew memory of him recorded the fact that he had not left his home in the region of Haran on the basis of purely human considerations. Of all of the peoples on the move in the second millenium B.C., Abraham was chosen from among them to be a special instrument of God. Through him the Lord would make the nation Israel, and by means of him, God would bring blessing to all the people on the face of the earth. In this promise of God to the historical chieftain Abraham, Israel later saw the beginning of its life with the Lord and the reason for its existence on the earth. Israel, the descendants of Abraham, were to be the means whereby God bestowed his favor on all mankind.

Explicit in this promise of God, too, was the gift of a land to Abraham's descendants. He was to leave behind country and kindred and home to journey to a land which God would show him, a land whose name he knew not, but nevertheless a land promised to his people by the Lord.

There were three parts to the original promise to the Hebrew patriarch: the promise of descendants who would become a great nation, of a land to call their own, and of a mission to be God's source of blessing for the world. Added to this, there is in the traditions concerning Abraham which were gathered together in priestly circles, a fourth element in the promise. This is the assurance that God will establish with Israel a special relationship, a covenant, in which he will be their God and they shall be his people. (Gen. 17:7-8.)

Now all of these historical facts and religious traditions concerning Abraham seem, on the face of it, matters of complete indifference to us. And yet, here lies the foundation of our understanding of the story of the whole Bible.

With his promise to Abraham, probably sometime in the eighteenth century B.C., God, the Lord of the universe and the ruler of history, has spoken a word into the life of mankind. But this is no idle word. It is the affirmation of the Bible that God's word is an active power. It is a power which shapes the course of history. It is a power which moves history forward and brings about events.

When God gives his promise to Abraham, he releases into history a vital force, which will now become determinative of the events following after it. This promise of God to the Hebrew patriarch will now shape the happenings in man's world and move them forward until the promise is fulfilled. God's word in the Bible never returns to him without accomplishing that which God has spoken:

> For as the rain and the snow come down from heaven,
>   and return not thither but water the earth,
> making it bring forth and sprout,
>   giving seed to the sower and bread to the eater,
> so shall my word be that goes forth from my mouth;
>   it shall not return to me empty,
> but it shall accomplish that which I purpose,
>   and prosper in the thing for which I sent it.
>   (Isa. 55:10-11; cf. 45:23.)

21

When God speaks, his word runs forward through the course of history until it accomplishes God's purpose. When God utters a promise into history, he always brings that promise to pass (Isa. 46:11).

For this reason, scholars employ for the biblical history the German word *Heilsgeschichte*, which is translated "saving history." This term points to the fact that the biblical history is not like any other history, but rather that it is a record of events in which a divine action is taking place. God is on the move in the Bible. He is working toward a goal. When he speaks his word into the realm of time and space, he thereby declares his intention. And then he does not rest until he has fulfilled his intention and brought history to the goal which he has set for it. The instrument of his working is his word. The word which he speaks is fulfilled. In short, the word and action of God are synonymous, and what God says, he does.

God speaks a word to Abraham. He injects a promise into the course of human history. And everything which follows after this promise to Abraham in Genesis can be understood in terms of it. The whole biblical story is the record of how God fulfills his promise to the Hebrew patriarch. In terms of five verses in the first book of the Old Testament (Gen. 12:1-3; 17:7-8), we can lay the foundation for understanding the entire scriptures.

Here is the crucial beginning, and the rest of our discussion will be ultimately concerned with the way God's word works in history. But first we must turn to examine why the Old Testament understands this promise to have been given to Abraham in the first place. Why did God find it necessary to utter this word in the second millennium B.C?

CHAPTER II

The Reason for the Promise:
The Primeval History in Genesis
(Read Genesis 1-11)

The stories of creation and of man's primeval beginnings in the first eleven chapters of the book of Genesis were not written primarily to explain how the world came to be. The Hebrews had little interest in the philosophical question of origin. Rather these stories were gathered together and set down to explain why Israel had to be. They were intended to show why it was necessary for God to enter into history and to begin a divine action by giving his promise to Abraham. We can see this quite clearly if we examine the contents and arrangement of these ancient materials.

There is no doubt that in the two creation stories which we find in Genesis, the first (Gen. 1:1-2:4a) from the sixth century B.C., and the second (Gen. 2:4b-25) from the tenth century B.C., man occupies an exalted position in the order of creation. In the first chapter of Genesis, he is seen as the goal of creation, as the result of a special act of God's deliberation, as an expression of the divine nature, and as the recipient of a closer relationship to the Lord than any work of creation.

23

Male and female, it is said, are created in the image of God:

> Then God said, "Let us make man in our image, after our like-ness; and let them have dominion over the fish of the sea, and over the birds of the air, and over the cattle, and over all the earth, and over every creeping thing that creeps upon the earth." So God created man in his own image, in the image of God he created him; male and female he created them. (Gen. 1:26-27.)

On the basis of the Hebrew terminology used to express this thought in Gen. 1:26-27, it is very likely that the priestly writer of this ancient passage had in mind man's physical and bodily similarity to the inhabitants of the divine realm. The reading in the ancient Hebrew is not "the image of God," but "the image of the 'elohim," the latter being the inhabitants of the heavenly court. And the words for "image" and "like-ness" throughout the Old Testament consistently refer to material representations and physical forms.

The author of this passage, then, is saying that the pattern for man was drawn from the divine realm. He does not say directly that man looks like God. Man never knows what God looks like in the Old Testament, for God always hides himself, with a cloud and fire and darkness, as at Mount Sinai (Exod. 19), with dazzling light, as in the Psalms (Ps. 104:2), or among his heavenly court, as here in Gen. 1. Man cannot connect his form directly with that of God's. The uniqueness of God is always preserved.

And yet, there seems little doubt here that in the thought of this first creation story, God is not to be thought of an-thropomorphically, that is, as having the form of man, but that man is to be thought of theomorphically, as having the form of God. As it is put in Ezek. 28:12, man is "the signet of perfection, full of wisdom and perfect in beauty." Therefore when Ezekiel (ch. 1) or Isaiah (ch. 6) or Daniel (7:9) are granted their prophetic visions of God, the deity is revealed to them as having something like a human form, not because they create God in man's image, but because man has been created in God's. Man's physical nature shares in some way in the glory and perfection of the Lord's being.

Certainly this does not exhaust the meaning of the image of God in the Old Testament. Man is given the image in order that he may exercise dominion over the earth (Gen. 1:26, 28). Just as God is Lord over all creation, so man is made lord over all life on earth, exercising his sovereignty on behalf of and in the name of God. This would imply, then, that man is made in God's image for a divine purpose and that man fulfills that purpose only in so far as he sets his own sovereignty over life in the service of God.

Yet, we must remain somewhat vague about the point, because the Old Testament is vague about it. The priestly author of the first chapter of Genesis knows no connection of the image with man's sinlessness. The image of God is mentioned in only two other places in the Old Testament. In Gen. 5:3, Adam passes the image on to his son Seth, and in Gen. 9:6, the image is still present in man at the time of Noah. The image has not been lost in the fall of man, and it is passed down from one generation to the next. There is no statement in the Old Testament concerning the effect of sin on the image of God.

That which is evident in this first Creation story in Genesis is that man, as created by God, is a glorious creature, beautiful in his form, lordly in his dominion over the earth, favored in his relationship to his creator. Far from being an insignificant

25

speck lost in a vast universe, man is, in the thought of our author, the exalted and glorious high point of all of God's good creation. And man is given this high station by the God who has created him.

The portrayal of man in the second chapter of Genesis is no less noble, despite the fact that this Creation story is now focused upon the intimate associations of man's life. No longer is there an interest in cosmogony and the creation of the world as a whole. All focuses on man, who is the center of the Creation, and nothing is mentioned which does not concern man's needs.

Indeed, man is so important in Gen. 2 that God takes infinite pains to satisfy his every necessity. The original waterless waste of the world is turned into an oasis, which man can till and cultivate. Man is set in the midst of a garden and given every tree which is pleasant to see and productive of food to eat. Man is given dominion over the animals by the fact that he is allowed to name them. And finally, man's loneliness and isolation are broken by the creation of a wife to be with him.

The woman whom God creates for man is intended to complement his being, and the point of Gen. 2:18-20 is that woman is man's essential supplement. She is that which completes his being, which makes him fully man. In ancient Hebrew thought a man could not be whole without a wife.

While man ('adam) is created from the dust of the ground ('adamah) and thus has an intimate relationship with it (Gen. 2:7), the woman is made from the rib of the man and is only indirectly related to the soil. But in the fact that woman is taken from man and was originally one flesh with him, the Hebrew sees the basis of the physical attraction of

the sexes. They were originally one flesh, and after the creation of the wife, they long to become one again. This longing
is finally satisfied in the unity of marital love and the subse-
quent merging of their two lives in the person of their child.
Far from being viewed as evil in the Old Testament, the
sexual life of man and wife is considered a gift of God (cf. Ps.
127:3-5; 128:3-4). And when Adam for the first time knows
his wife, his response is ecstatic joy: "This at last is bone of
my bones and flesh of my flesh." (Gen. 2:23.)

Taken as a whole, the portrayal of man which we have in
this second chapter of Genesis is a good and healthy one.
Life in all of its facets is affirmed, and man is created to live
it to the full. He is to till the good soil which God has given
him, surrounded by God's gifts of wife and children, joyful
in the blessings bestowed upon him by a thoughtful and
loving Creator. As in Gen. 1:31, the author of this chapter
sees that the creation of God is very good, and it is not
overstatement to say that the Hebrew simply revels in its
goodness. No view of the religious life could be further
from asceticism than is that of the Old Testament.

In both of these creation stories, however, man's relationship to God is clearly defined as one of complete dependence.
In Gen. 2:7, God personally creates man, in the most intimate fashion. Like a potter working with a lump of clay, he
takes some of the dust of the ground and mixes it with water,
and then he shapes man in his hands, until man has a form
(cf. Job 10:8-11; Ps. 139:13-15). But man does not yet have
life. There he lies, a lump of clay in the hands of his Creator.
Then God breathes the breath of life into man's nostrils, and
man becomes a living being. He has life only because God
chooses to give it to him. He breathes only because God has

breathed into him. His life is not inherent within his physical body. He does not exist in his own right, but solely as a creature, sustained by the grace of his Creator. If God holds his breath, man will return to dead physical matter (Ps. 104: 29; Job 34:14-15). Man is completely dependent for his life on the will of his Maker.

In Gen. 1, man is dependent on God for the structure of his world. In the beginning, we are told, the earth was nothing but a dark and watery chaos: "The earth was without form and void, and darkness was upon the face of the deep; and the Spirit of God was moving over the face of the waters" (Gen. 1:2). The nature of the creation was to bring order into this disorder. God accomplished this by limiting the chaos and holding it in check. The chaotic deep or waters were bounded by being held above the firmament and below the earth (Gen. 1:6-7; cf. Job 38:8-11; Ps. 104:9; Prov. 8:29). The darkness was separated from the light and given the boundaries of night (Gen. 1:4-5). Through his creative word, God pushed back evil disorder and established an order in the world which made it habitable (Isa. 45:18).

And yet, God did not eliminate the forces of chaos. They can still threaten the order of the world. As Job says, Leviathan, which is another name for the chaotic waters, can be roused (Job 3:8). The great deep can burst forth again, as it did in the flood at the time of Noah (Gen. 7:11).

The only thing which prevents the world from returning to chaos is the power of its Creator. Only because God has set a guard over Leviathan (Job 7:12) is the structure of man's world preserved. Only because God promises that the deep will never again burst forth is mankind freed from the threat of chaotic annihilation (Gen. 9:11, 15). If God with-

28

draws the protection of his creative word of power, the earth will again become waste and void (Jer. 4:23). It is only because "God is our refuge and strength" that we need not fear when the chaotic waters roar (Ps. 46:1-3). Man in the Old Testament is completely dependent on God for his life and the order of his world. God is, in other words, Lord over man's existence.

The stories which follow in Gen. 3-11 show the consequences of man's rebellion against dependence on this Lordship. They are made up of ancient legends and incomplete parts of myths. But they are put together in such a way that they portray imaginatively the way in which all men have walked and show the reason for the historical call of Abraham.

The sin of Eve in the garden of Eden in Gen. 3 is her attempt to escape her need for God. She is created to rely on her Creator, but in her conversation with the serpent, she is led to step outside this relationship of dependency and to evaluate and discuss God's motives. She becomes aware of the fact that she may judge God to be wrong.

But the serpent said to the woman, "You will not die. For God knows that when you eat of [the fruit of the tree in the midst of the garden] your eyes will be opened, and you will be like God, knowing good and evil" (Gen. 3:4-5).

Eve's temptation is to rely on herself rather than on God. If she eats of the fruit of the forbidden tree, she will know all mysteries and all knowledge. She will be the master of her own fate, the determiner of her own destiny. She reaches out to grasp this power which belongs to God alone, and she gives of the fruit to her husband so that he, too, is involved in her rebellion.

Here we have masterfully portrayed for us man in all of his glory and misery. Here is man—titanic, glorious man—who wants to rule the world. And yet, after he eats the forbidden fruit, he must hastily and shamefully sew fig leaves together to hide his own nakedness (Gen. 3:7). And here is man—sovereign, independent man—who, when he is asked to take responsibility for that which he has done, can only try to shift the blame on to someone else:

> The man said, "The woman whom thou gavest to be with me, she gave me fruit of the tree, and I ate." Then the Lord God said to the woman, "What is this that you have done?" The woman said, "The serpent beguiled me, and I ate." (Gen. 3:12-13.)

By trying to shake off their dependence on their Lord, Adam and Eve become weak and pitiful. When they violate their relationship to God, they lose their strength and glory.

The judgment which God pronounces on this couple for their rebellion against him disrupts every intimate relationship of their lives. Their tie with one another is no longer one of ecstatic joy, but marked by shame and the necessity for hiding their sexuality. The woman, whose created function is to join flesh with her husband by bearing him children in marriage, now has that function threatened by difficulty and pain in childbirth (Gen. 3:16). The man, who was taken from the soil and created by God to tend it (Gen. 2:15), now finds that the ground fights back at him and produces thorns and thistles. Only by unremitting sweat and toil will he secure his food (Gen. 3:17-19). And after his labor, his end will be, as God had warned him (Gen. 2:17), death (Gen. 3:19).

The goodness of life which God had given to man in creation is here totally disrupted.

What is more, man's intimate relationship with God is broken by his rebellion. This is the God who had shaped man personally and looked after his every need. Man must now hide from God's presence in fear at the sound of God's voice (Gen. 3:8-10). Indeed, man is driven from the garden of Eden, and cherubim and a flaming sword are placed to guard its entrance (Gen. 3:24). To put it in other words, man has trodden a way which he himself cannot retrace. The guards are there, and there is nothing man can do to get rid of them. Only God can remove them. Man has reached a point of no return.

Yet, this judgment is not God's final word to Adam and Eve. Before he drives them from the garden, he also shows them his mercy. He sits down and makes clothes for them out of skins, in order that their life together may be possible (Gen. 3:21). And we are told in Gen. 4:1, that they are given a child "with the help of the Lord." In the midst of his anger, God manifests his love. In fact, we shall find throughout this primeval history that for each act of God's judgment there is an act of corresponding mercy, and that the God of these Genesis stories is above all a God of love.

The rebellion which Adam and Eve have initiated grows increasingly worse in the stories that follow, however, and at every juncture, the judgment on it is more severe. When Cain kills his brother Abel, brotherly hatred enters history, and the disruption which was present between the parents now spreads through the whole family (Gen. 4). The farmer Cain therefore not only fights with the soil, but is completely alienated from it, forced to become a fugitive and wanderer on the earth (Gen. 4:12), hidden from the face of God (Gen. 4:14, 16). And yet, here, too, God's mercy is present and Cain is a protected fugitive. God puts a mark on him in order that no one will slay him (Gen. 4:15). Though driven from the presence of his God, Cain is not beyond God's mercy.

At this juncture in our story, we read of the growth of culture (Gen. 4:17-24). There is the mention of the first city, of cattle herders, and of musicians. But when the smith is introduced, the result of his work is Lamech's terrible sword of vengeance (Gen. 4:23-24). The disruption caused by man's rebellion has now spread through mankind. Lamech is the epitomy of man's hatred for man.

Indeed, it is the purpose of our author to show that the disruption of man's sin even invades the divine realm. To do so, he introduces a part of a very old myth (Gen. 6:1-4). In this myth, the sons of the gods take to themselves for wives the daughters of men. The result of this union are the Nephilim, the giants, a demonic race of supermen, in which the divine vitality is mixed with the human. These Nephilim have the possibility of living forever and therefore of challenging God's sovereignty. God's judgment upon them is to limit their life span to 120 years and to relegate them to the realm of mortal men (Gen. 6:3).

But the point of all this is to show that man is thoroughly corrupted. His rebellion has spread so that it even invades the heavenly realm. As it is put so well in Gen. 6:5-6, "every imagination of the thoughts of his heart was only evil continually. And the Lord was sorry that he had made man on the earth, and it grieved him to his heart." The one recourse left to God is to blot out the creation. The flood becomes his judgment on a world which has rebelled against him (Gen. 6-7). The waters of chaos are released from above the firmament and from below the earth (Gen. 7:11), and the world returns to its primeval state of watery waste and void.

Yet, here, too, God's mercy prevails. Noah and his family are saved in the ark, along with representatives of every living creature. And God himself even shuts the door of the ark after Noah (Gen. 7:16), just to make sure it is tightly sealed. When his wrath is expended, God "remembers" Noah (Gen. 8:1) and carefully restores the order of creation, promising that the seasons and harvest and day and night will never cease (Gen. 8:22) and that the primeval chaos will never again rise to threaten the existence of the world (Gen. 9:8-17). Despite man's continuing sin after the flood (Gen. 8:21; 9:20-25), God's love is not overcome.

At the tower of Babel (Gen. 11:1-9), mankind is brought to its ultimate rebellion. All nations unite together in a co-operative venture. Their unity would seem good on the face of it, but their goal is still revolt. "Come, let us build ourselves a city," they say, "and a tower with its top in the heavens, and let us make a name for ourselves, lest we be scattered abroad upon the face of the whole earth." (Gen. 11:4.) Here no longer is man a lump of clay, completely dependent on his Creator. He is a rebel storming the heights of heaven in order to create his own glory. His perfection, he thinks, is not his likeness to God but his ability to replace God. His task, he deems, is not to serve God, but to make God unnecessary. From Eden to Babel, mankind has not learned a thing. In his judgment at Babel, God therefore disperses mankind throughout the earth and confuses his language, in order that man may never again co-operatively

33

challenge the Lord of the world (Gen. 11:7-9). The possibility of human relationships is replaced by confusion. Revolt against God leads inevitably to the disruption of human society.

Seemingly the primeval history ends here, for there follows in Gen. 11:10 ff. only a list of the descendants of Shem. In short, the judgment pronounced on mankind at the tower of Babel appears to be God's final word, and for the first time in this primeval history there is no covering mercy. God apparently has deserted the human race and left it to its evil devices. Mankind has walked the irreversible way of rebellion, and God has abandoned him to destruction. We, in short, have fallen like Adam, for Adam is every man. We have now been irrevocably cut off from the good life given us in creation. "All we like sheep have gone astray." We have been judged by God; we have been scattered abroad on the face of the earth. We have lost the power to communicate with our fellowmen. Our life is now one of pain and toil and guilt, ending in nothing but the obliteration of death.

But to man's rebellion God answers with his love. Sometime around the eighteenth century B.C., God enters into history and calls a man named Abraham out of Mesopotamia. To Abraham God gives a promise, the promise that through Abraham's descendants, he will once more bestow his blessing on all mankind. All men have been judged by God, but God now graciously begins an action in history which will restore all men to his favor. From Eden to Babel, man has run away from God. God now begins an action to bring him home again. We can perhaps begin to understand why Matthew states in the first verse of his gospel that Jesus Christ is the descendant of Abraham. It is with that Hebrew patriarch that God begins the history of salvation which is finally to reach its culmination in the Cross and Resurrection.

We must be careful to avoid a misunderstanding at this point, however. The author who put the promise to Abraham into writing had no divine foreknowledge of Jesus Christ. He was not granted some mystical vision which allowed him to gaze across the centuries and to foresee their outcome. But he was granted the word of God as it came down to him in Hebrew tradition. That word he recorded faithfully. He perhaps did not understand its full meaning. He did not know in what way it would be fulfilled. He knew only that God had spoken and that God would keep his promise. But there is much more we must understand before we can intelligently affirm his faith.

Chapter III

The Working Out of the Promise:
The Narratives of Genesis-Joshua

1. THE PROMISE AS THE BACKGROUND OF THE PATRIARCHAL NARRATIVES

(Read Genesis 12-50)

To the lay reader, the stories of Gen. 12-50 often seem like a conglomeration of irrelevant legends having little to do with faith. Indeed, these tales appear to have a decidedly secular nature, and there are pages and pages, especially in the traditions about Jacob, where God is not mentioned at all. The reader finds accounts in Genesis of rape and murder, or brotherly strife and jealousy, of two unsatisfied wives fighting over a man, of malice and cunning between relatives. These are mixed, on the reverse side of the ledger, with incidents of love and forgiveness and tenderness. But the whole seems a history, however frank its tone, in which God is peculiarly absent.

In the attempt to make these Genesis narratives relevant to our religion, therefore, we often turn them into moral lessons.

Joseph's troubles with his brothers become jumping-off points for discussions on family relations. Abraham's unselfishness or kindness or belief is set before us as an example.

These moralizing attempts are not wholly without justification. Certainly the Old Testament is realistic about life, and these patriarchal narratives may portray our motives and ambitions and feelings more incisively than we would otherwise care to admit. Moreover, a faith such as Abraham's in the promise of God is truly exemplary, as the New Testament points out to us (Heb. 11:8-12, 17-21; 6:13-15; John 8:39; Jas. 2:21-24; Rom. 4:18-21).

But if moral lessons and examples for life are all that we find in the Genesis stories, then we shall have missed the central point of this portion of our Bible. Further, we shall have placed in the path of our faith terrible stumbling blocks, for in many of the incidents concerning the patriarchs, it is difficult to concede their morality.

That which we must recognize here, as in the primeval history, is that these stories grow out of God's promise to Abraham, a promise which is subsequently renewed both for Isaac (Gen. 26) and for Jacob (Gen. 28:1-17). The central character of these stories is not the patriarchs, but God himself, and the plot of the drama concerns the way in which God keeps his word.

Let us consider just a few examples illustrative of this central theme. In the traditions concerning Abraham, we are confronted continually with God's efforts to provide Abraham with descendants, and the stories are given dramatic intensity by the obstacles set in the way of the fulfillment of this part of the promise.

In Gen. 12:10-19, we find a tale in which a famine forces

Abraham into Egypt (cf. 20; 26:1-11). Since Abraham's wife, Sarah, is a beautiful woman, the patriarch fears that the Egyptians may kill him in order to have his wife. God's promise to make Abraham the father of a great nation would then remain unfulfilled. To avoid such an exigency, Abraham claims that Sarah is his sister. This, however, helps little, for when the Pharaoh takes Sarah into his harem, God's promise seems similarly doomed. God overcomes the obstacle to his word by intervening in the affair and by afflicting Pharaoh and his house with a number of plagues as a warning. The Lord works actively here in this story to assure the success of his promise.

The greatest obstacle to the fulfillment of the divine word undoubtedly then is the fact that both Abraham and his wife are old and past the age of childbearing (Gen. 17:17; 18:11). How is Abraham to be the progenitor of a people when he and his wife are incapable of having children? Sarah herself laughs at the absurdity of such a prospect (Gen. 18:12-15). But the constant emphasis of Genesis is that God's word cannot be defeated. In the spring of the year, the Lord returns to "visit" Sarah and she bears Isaac to her aged husband (Gen. 18:10; 21:1-7). The promise of descendants to the patriarch is now on its way to fulfillment.

Then God himself throws up the most difficult barrier to faith. We are told in Gen. 22 that the Lord commands Abraham to take Isaac to the land of Moriah and there to sacrifice him upon a mountain as a burnt offering to the Lord. God has given Abraham the first of his descendants, his only son, and now he would take him away. That the patriarch must have been torn between his trust in the promise of God and his fatherly impulse to save his son in disobedience of God goes, of course, without saying. But the exemplary nature of

Abraham's faith is that he holds fast to both the promise and the commandment of the Lord. He goes forth to sacrifice Isaac, as the God of the promise has commanded. Though all circumstances war against it, Abraham trusts that God knows what he is doing. And this trust is vindicated when the Lord provides an animal to take Isaac's place in the sacrifice. Abraham proves himself worthy to be the bearer of God's word, as is indicated at the end of the story when the promise is renewed (Gen. 22:15-18).

This same dramatic struggle between God's word and the obstacles to its fulfillment forms the major motif throughout the rest of Genesis. Everywhere there are difficulties. Isaac's wife, Rebekah, is barren (Gen. 25:21), as is also Rachel, the wife of Jacob (Gen. 29:31). Jacob's life is threatened by his brother Esau (Gen. 27:41-45), who hates him because he has stolen his birthright and his blessing (Gen. 27:36, 41). When Jacob takes refuge with Laban in Haran, Laban would halt his return to the promised land (Gen. 31:22 ff.). And when Jacob escapes the clutches of Laban, he is confronted again by the wrath of his brother (Gen. 32). At every turn these patriarchs, who are to be the fathers of a great nation which will inherit the land of Canaan, are threatened by difficulties which would seem to make it impossible for God to keep his word to them. And throughout each story in Genesis, it is this word of God which forms the dramatic background of the narrative.

That it costs the patriarchs to be the instruments of God's word we are allowed to experience through these stories. Not one of us who has a child can escape something of the feelings of Abraham when he raised his knife to slaughter Isaac. And the story of Jacob wrestling with that mysterious man in the dark beside the river Jabbok (Gen. 32:23-32) somehow becomes typical of the struggle to which faith in God's word subjects us. "I will not let you go, unless you bless me," Jacob cries out. Jacob is given his blessing, but he emerges from his encounter with God, limping. God does not desert those to whom he has made a promise, but the struggle of faith at times leaves them wounded.

One of the most subtle presentations of this struggle of the patriarchs is to be found in the enigmatic story of Dinah and Shechem, the son of Hamor, in Gen. 34. Here we find an ancient legend which seems to have no connection with that which precedes or follows it. But surely the story is to be understood as a temptation to Jacob's faith in God's promise of a land for his descendants. The Hivite Hamor offers to let his people intermarry with the Hebrews:

Make marriages with us; give your daughters to us, and take our daughters for yourselves. You shall dwell with us; and the land shall be open to you; dwell and trade in it, and get property in it. (Gen. 34:9.)

In short, the temptation offered to Jacob here is to possess the promised land by the natural means of intermarriage and settlement, to fulfill by human means the promise given by a divine Lord. Jacob confronts a temptation common to the man of faith: the attempt to fulfill God's promises for him, before God is ready to fulfill them. The answer of Jacob's sons to this test is to wipe out those who have tempted their father.

Abraham and Isaac and Jacob never do themselves possess the promised land in their lifetimes. They are given the land, but they never own it, for the promise given to them is postponed in its fulfillment until all of Israel may participate in it, in the conquest under Joshua. Thus, the authors of Genesis are careful to point out that the Canaanites are still in Palestine and that the land still belongs to them. Further, throughout Genesis, the land is for Abraham a "land of sojournings." He wanders through Canaan, but he is only a pilgrim and a sojourner there, until the time comes when the Lord shall give the land to his descendants.

Only in one way do the patriarchs themselves take possession of the land—in death. This is the point of Gen. 23. In that chapter, Abraham purchases by very legal means from the Hittites a field called Ephron in Machpelah, which is to the east of Mamre. He buys the field for a burial ground, and here each of the patriarchs, with his wife, is buried. In this one way, in death, the patriarchs themselves take possession of the land the Lord has promised their descendants. It is a foretaste, the first fruits, as it were, of the final fulfillment of God's promise in the conquest under Joshua.

The patriarchs are, then, actually instruments of God's future. It is to them that God gives the promise and it is through them that God works his will. But the goal of God's working lies in the future, in a time beyond the patriarchs.

This can be seen very clearly when we consider, finally, the Joseph stories. These tales in chapters 37-50 make up the longest cycle of tradition in Genesis, and yet their whole point can be summarized in one sentence. Joseph is sold by his brothers into Egypt and is finally given his position of authority under the Pharaoh in order that God may preserve alive the descendants of Abraham for the fulfillment of his word. This is stated explicitly in Gen. 45:4-8:

So Joseph said to his brothers, "Come near to me, I pray you."

41

And they came near. And he said, "I am your brother, Joseph, whom you sold into Egypt. And now do not be distressed, or angry with yourselves, because you sold me here; for God sent me before you to preserve life. For the famine has been in the land these two years; and there are yet five years in which there will be neither plowing nor harvest. And God sent me before you to preserve for you a remnant on earth, and to keep alive for you many survivors. So it was not you who sent me here, but God; and he has made me a father to Pharaoh, and lord of all his house and ruler over all the land of Egypt."

Had the Hebrews died from famine in the time of Joseph, God's promise could never have been fulfilled, and Joseph is an instrument for insuring that it will be (cf. Ps. 105:16-17).

God moves forward in the book of Genesis, guiding, leading, protecting his own. Jacob calls him "the God who has led me all my life long to this day" (Gen. 48:15). In all the mundane affairs of the patriarchal narratives, we see the Lord actively engaged. He it is who "remembers" Rachel and opens her womb (Gen. 30:22). He is the one who protects Jacob and brings him back home from Haran (Gen. 31:3, 13, 24). He is the God who gives Joseph his spirit in order that Joseph may be released from prison (Gen. 41:16, 38 ff.).

But behind this activity lies the purpose of God, the purpose to fulfill his promise. And before he dies in Egypt, Joseph affirms anew that the promise will be kept: "And Joseph said to his brothers, 'I am about to die; but God will visit you, and bring you up out of this land to the land which he swore to Abraham, to Isaac, and to Jacob'" (Gen. 50:24). It is the word of God to the patriarchs which forms the background of their stories. And it is to the fulfillment of the same word that the end of Genesis looks forward.

2. "AND I WILL MAKE OF YOU A GREAT NATION": THE CREATION OF ISRAEL

(Read Exodus 1-15:22)

We now know with reasonable historical certainty that several thousand Hebrews were brought up out of the land of Egypt some time around 1280 B.C. Undoubtedly these people of the Exodus had come to Egypt at different times and from different backgrounds, and they were members of varying clans and races. But all came eventually to be parts of Israel and thus are included in Israel's story.

We are told in the first chapter of the book of Exodus that the descendants of Israel grew numerous in Egypt (Exod. 1:7) and that when there arose a new king over Egypt, who did not know Joseph, these people were forced to labor on the royal construction gangs in the cities of Pithom and Raamses (Exod. 1:8-11).

The authenticity of this tradition is supported by several historical and archaeological facts. First of all, the city of Raamses was rebuilt and again made the capital of the empire under the Pharaohs Sethos I (ca. 1309-1290 B.C.) and Ramesses II (ca. 1290-1224 B.C.), and both of these Pharaohs were engaged in extensive building operations. Again, the city of Raamses was called by that name only until the eleventh century B.C., after which it was referred to as Tanis.

These dates fit in perfectly with the evidence which we have concerning the Hebrews' whereabouts in this period. According to the stele of Marniptah, Israel was in Palestine by 1220 B.C. But we know that the Israelites could not have left Egypt before 1300 B.C., because they encountered both Edom and Moab in the wilderness (Num. 20; 21), and neither of these two kingdoms was established before that time. That at least some of Israel's tribes were in Egypt at all is supported by the fact that Egyptian names are prevalent in early Israel, especially among the tribe of Levi, Moses and Aaron being two outstanding examples.

Therefore it is reasonable to conclude that Sethos I and Ramesses II were the Pharaohs of Israel's oppression, and that the exodus from Egypt took place between 1300 and 1220 B.C. Allowing for the time in the wilderness and the conquest, we can surmise that the Hebrews escaped from Egypt about the year 1280 B.C.

It is the witness throughout the Old Testament that the Lord effected this escape. Not only is this stated in Israel's most ancient creeds and by Israel's earlier prophets, it is affirmed by Israel's historians and celebrated by the psalmists. No event in Israel's past is more universally remembered in the Old Testament than the Exodus. And no one action of God is seen as more important than his redemption of the Hebrews from Egypt.

Indeed, because the Lord wrought this event, he is forever after in the Old Testament identified as "the Lord your God from the land of Egypt" (Hos. 12:9), and to worship other gods, Israel had to claim that they had effected this deliverance (Exod. 32:4; I Kings 12:28). The God of Israel and this deliverance were indissolubly remembered together.

This connection of God with his actions is typical throughout the Bible. The biblical writers never think of God in abstract terms, as being transcendant or immanent, omniscient or omnipotent. They think of God in terms of what he has done, and they identify their God by his action. As God is "the Lord your God from the land of Egypt" in the Old Testament, so he is "the God and Father of our Lord Jesus

44

Christ" in the New, and by describing God in terms of the events he has wrought, the nature of God is made clear. The biblical accounts of God's actions tell us of his nature, and by grasping the fullness of these accounts, we know God as he truly is.

It was in their redemption from Egypt that the Israelites most fully came to understand the nature of the Lord. For one thing, he revealed his name, Yahweh, to them (Exod. 3:13-15; 6:3), and this meant that they could now invoke him freely and call upon him in prayer. No longer need they deal with a power whose identity they knew not. No longer was God a "someone in the great somewhere." Now he was a personal Lord, to whom they could call and respond. His name was Yahweh. He was an I for Israel's Thou.

The Exodus also revealed to Israel that Yahweh was a God of power. He summoned all of the forces of nature to persuade the Pharaoh to let his people go, and the might of Egypt was as nothing before his sovereign will. Just as in the New Testament, the resurrection of Christ is seen as the revelation of his Father's power over all forces, both historical and cosmic (cf. Rom. 8:31-39), so in the Old Testament, the Exodus is seen as the revelation of Yahweh's power over both nature and history. The psalmists therefore celebrate the Exodus as an earth-shaking manifestation of might:

> When Israel went forth from Egypt,
>   the house of Jacob from a people of strange language,
>
> . . . .
>
> The sea looked and fled,
>   Jordan turned back.
> The mountains skipped like rams,
>   the hills like lambs.

What ails you, O sea, that you flee?
　O Jordan, that you turn back?
O mountains, that you skip like rams?
　O hills, like lambs?
Tremble, O earth, at the presence of the Lord,
　at the presence of the God of Jacob,
who turns the rock into a pool of water,
　the flint into a spring of water.

(Ps. 114; cf. 135.)

This means that the Exodus is ever after a source of comfort to Israel. He now knows that his God is unconquerable and that therefore there is no situation in which he needs to be afraid. Though Israel be faced with superior odds in warfare (Deut. 7:17-19), or yoked by an exile's slavery (Isa. 10:24-27; 11:16), though he be confronted with a task that seems impossible (Hag. 2:4-5), or a situation which holds no hope (Jer. 32:16 ff.), Israel is to remember the Exodus and to trust in the power of his God to deliver him. Just as, in the New Testament, the Resurrection is a source of certain hope for the future (cf. I Pet. 1:3-4), so in the Old Testament the Exodus is a like source of comfort.

Primarily, however, Israel saw in God's redemption from Egypt the revelation of his marvelous love. As the Israelites looked back to their deliverance from "the house of bondage," they could find nothing in themselves which made them worthy of such deliverance. They were not a numerous people or a great one, like the contemporary Egyptians or Hittites. Indeed, they were nothing more than a comparatively small group of slave laborers. And yet, Yahweh singled them out from among all of the peoples of the earth to dwell with them (Exod. 29:46) and to make them "a people of his own

46

possession" (Deut. 4:20). He plucked them out of bondage and broke the bars of their yoke and made them walk erect (Lev. 26:13). He took the trouble to deliver them and them alone. In its remembrance of his deed Israel could do nothing but confess that God had acted out of love: "It was not because you were more in number than any other people that the Lord set his love upon you and chose you, for you were the fewest of all peoples; but it is because the Lord loves you" (Deut. 7:7-8).

It was this love which for the first time made the Hebrews a people. Now they were no longer separate clans and wanderers, each pursuing its own way. Now they were no longer different families and races, facing their separate destinies as best they could. Now they were one group, one people, plucked out of the bondage of historical circumstances by a common, shared redemptive act, and set into the freedom of the wilderness for a purpose which they as yet knew not. They had all been redeemed together. And from the moment of their redemption on, they shared a common destiny and a common life. In short, God's deliverance of the Hebrews from Egypt was his creation of the people Israel, and from this time forward, these Hebrews considered themselves a nation. They were not yet a twelve-tribed nation. That amphictyonic structure developed only after their entrance into Palestine. But they were the Israelite nation. They shared a common redemption and future.

Yahweh, then, was the Father of Israel (Isa. 63:16; Jer. 3:19). He had begotten Israel by delivering him from Egypt (Deut. 32:6, 10, 18; Isa. 64:8). And Israel from this time forth was called Yahweh's first-born son (Exod. 4:22; Jer. 31:9)!

The love which God manifested in his deliverance of his people was the love of a father for his child.

> When Israel was a child, I loved him,
> and out of Egypt I called my son.
> (Hos. 11:1.)

Yahweh it was who taught his child to walk (Hos. 11:3), who reared him up (Isa. 1:2) and cherished him (Jer. 31:20). The exodus from Egypt marked the deliverance of God's son. It is not surprising, then, that Matthew recalls this event in his story of Jesus Christ (Matt. 2:14-15), for as we shall see, our Lord becomes finally the Israel of faith.

Israel, however, could not delude himself by thinking that God had delivered him for no purpose. He was not a son created to go his own way, unmindful of the Father who had begotten him or of the purposes of that Father. Yahweh had set his love upon Israel for a specific reason, and this son was brought forth in order that he might serve his Father. "Israel is my first-born son, and I say to you, 'Let my son go that he may serve me.'" (Exod. 4:22-23.) Israel is the chosen people in the Old Testament, chosen not in order to enjoy God's privilege, but to be the instrument of his will: "For to me the people of Israel are servants, they are my servants whom I brought forth out of the land of Egypt: I am the Lord your God" (Lev. 25:55). Like the Son of God in the New Testament, Israel must "work the works of him who sent" him (John 9:4; 17:4).

To put it in other words, the unmerited love of God which Israel experienced in the redemption from the house of bondage was not love for its own sake, but love for the sake of God, love given in order that Yahweh might work toward a goal, love bestowed for a specific divine purpose. It was free and unmerited love in that there was nothing about Israel which qualified him to receive such mercy. Israel might well ask in astonished gratitude, "Why should I be chosen?" But the unmerited nature of the love did not mean it was given without reason. The God of the Bible loves Israel, as he later loves his new Israel, the Church, precisely because he has a purpose.

This purpose for the redemptive act of the Exodus, Israel found once more in the promise to the patriarchs. God had delivered Israel because God remembered his covenant with Abraham, with Isaac, and with Jacob (Exod. 2:24). God brought Israel up out of Egypt, because he had promised to make him a nation. God set Israel free in the wilderness to start the march toward the promised land (Lev. 25:38; Deut. 6:23; Ps. 105).

It is because the Lord loves you, and is keeping the oath which he swore to your fathers, that the Lord has brought you out with a mighty hand, and redeemed you from the house of bondage, from the hand of Pharaoh king of Egypt. (Deut. 7:8.)

Included in this promise to the patriarchs, however, had been the oath to bring blessing on all nations through Israel, and this Israel saw as the ultimate reason for its own redemption and creation as a nation. God's son was born out of Egypt for God's purpose of redeeming all mankind. Israel was set free from the house of bondage to be the means whereby God would restore to men the good life that he had given them in creation. This good life they had lost by their rebellion, as we saw symbolized in the primeval history. In the event of the

Exodus, God continued to work to restore this good life to men.

In many parts of the Old Testament, therefore, the exodus from Egypt is seen as an act of creation, not only the creation of Israel, but an act in the creation of the world. When Israel crosses the Red Sea, it is considered that the chaotic deep is once again bounded, just as we saw it bounded in the story of Gen. 1 (Ps. 106:9; 114:3, 5). When God creates Israel, he begins literally to re-create his world, fashioning the means whereby rebellious men may be restored to the good life they have lost (Isa. 51:9-11).

God loves and chooses Israel in order that Israel may serve him, in order that through Israel he may bestow his love upon all. God loves Israel, because he loves all mankind (cf. I Tim. 2:3-4).

3. "AND I WILL ESTABLISH MY COVENANT BETWEEN ME AND YOU": THE NATURE OF ISRAEL'S SERVICE
(Read Exodus 15:22-24:11)

When the Israelites were delivered from bondage and set free in the wilderness, they had no idea how to conduct themselves in their new life. The picture we have in Exod. 16-18 is one of a confused multitude, uncertain in their trust of their new-found Redeemer, insecure away from the familiar scenes of Egypt, undecided as how to get along with one another and with their God. This situation was soon alleviated by the structuring of Israel's life in a covenant community. And it was this covenant, made at Mount Sinai with Yahweh, which defined the Israelites' relationship to one another and to their God. In short, it was the covenant which defined the nature of Israel's service to the Lord.

Primary to the covenant relationship was the fact that Yahweh was to be Israel's sole and sovereign Lord. He was to rule over his people and they were to serve him alone. Such is the essential meaning of the first four of the Ten Commandments (Exod. 20:3-11), and in all probability the Israelites heard commandments very similar to these from Moses at Mount Sinai. At the foot of that fearful peak Israel was placed before a choice. Having been delivered by Yahweh, he was now asked to serve Yahweh alone.

Israel's decision was not to be made in a vacuum. He had seen what Yahweh could do, how Yahweh had overcome the Egyptians and given victory over Amalek (Exod. 17:8-16), how he had led the Israelites in the desert and given them water and food (Exod. 15:22-16:36), how he had been their healer (Exod. 15:26) and proved himself constantly gracious. Israel's choice was therefore one to be made in the context of God's grace. Yahweh had taken the initiative. Israel was being asked to respond.

You have seen what I did to the Egyptians, and how I bore you on eagles' wings and brought you to myself. Now therefore, if you will obey my voice and keep my covenant, you shall be my own possession among all peoples; for all the earth is mine, and you shall be to me a kingdom of priests and a holy nation. (Exod. 19:4-6.)

The covenant which Israel was asked to make with Yahweh at Mount Sinai was no pact between equals, however. There was not to be a mutual give and take on both sides. Israel was not being asked to be God's partner. Israel was being asked to surrender, to give Yahweh full charge of his life, of his

51

loyalty, and of his destiny. This meant that if Israel entered into covenant relationship with the Lord, God's will forever after was to be the center of Israel's existence. And this fact had several implications for Israel's life in the world.

First of all, unlike all the surrounding cultures of the ancient Near East, Israel's task would no longer be one of adjusting to the natural environment. The ancient Sumerians and Assyrians and Egyptians and Canaanites found their gods in the phenomena of nature. And it was for the purpose of regulating and appeasing and harmonizing these phenomena that religion lived in these cultures. They found the center of their life in the forces of the natural world.

But Israel was now being asked to surrender to a power outside nature. God had revealed himself through the medium of historical events, and his will was not to be found in nature but in historical revelation, through the action and results of his spoken word. In short, the task of the people of God in both Old Testament and New is not to find God in the natural world, but to obey the voice of him who transcends nature as its Creator and Lord.

Secondly, if Israel entered into covenant relationship with Yahweh, he could not find the center of his life in any human culture. Yahweh had identified himself with no existing society. Rather, he had created a new one. And he now demanded of this people that they conform not to human laws and ethics and social standards and mores, but to his divine and transcendant will.

I am the Lord your God. You shall not do as they do in the land of Egypt, where you dwelt, and you shall not do as they do in the land of Canaan, to which I am bringing you. You shall not walk in their statutes. You shall do my ordinances and keep my statutes and walk in them. I am the Lord your God. (Lev. 18:2-4.)

Israel was to be holy, i.e., separate, as Yahweh was holy (Lev. 19:2), and he was to be like no other people on earth, for he was to be God's. Therefore, the people of God find the norm for their life in no human nation or social entity—not even in the American way of life—but in the will of God which transcends and differs from the cultural formulations of all human societies.

In the third place, if Israel entered into covenant relationship with Yahweh, Israel would pledge himself to live from that time on as a community. God wished to make a covenant not with individuals but with a people, a people united by a common obedience to him. There is no such thing in the Bible as a purely individual relationship to God, and those who would enter into covenant with the Lord must do so as a part of his community. Only by sharing a common life with other believers could each Israelite serve his God. He could not ignore or hate his fellow and at the same time love his Lord.

However, again, the basis of this community was not to be the will of man but the transcendant will of God. God made the laws for the communal life, he set up its structure, he ordered the relationships between members of the society. The last six of the Ten Commandments therefore deal with relations between men (Exod. 20:12-17) and are seen as expressions of the will of God for his people. Only in so far as God ruled over the communal life was it a true expression of his covenant will.

Because God was the ruler of the covenant society, however,

no one man within it could claim absolute authority. The kings who were later to rule in Israel could do so only if they were subservient to God, who was the true sovereign of Israel. And each man enjoyed equal rights before the divine ruler. No one could claim special privilege. No man could make his will the law for the total group. The government of the society lay in the hands of the God who transcended it.

This, then, was to be the nature of the covenant service into which Israel was asked to enter. And when Israel heard the demands which God had spoken to Moses on the mountain, Israel made his choice and dedicated himself to the Lord: "All the words which the Lord has spoken we will do" (Exod. 24:3; 19:7-8). Of his own free will, Israel agreed to be God's. There follows in Exod. 24:4-11, the description of the covenant ceremony.

It is instructive for the Christian to note the elements in this ceremony. First of all, there is a sacrifice, with half of the blood of the sacrifice thrown against the altar (vss. 5-6). Then follows the proclamation of the word, when Moses reads the covenant commandments to the people (vs. 7). Upon hearing the commandments, the people reaffirm their willingness to enter into the covenant relationship, whereupon the rest of the blood of the sacrifice is sprinkled upon the group, making them participants in the bond being effected (vss. 7-8). Finally, there follows a communion meal, in which Moses and the leaders of Israel eat and drink with God.

It is probably unnecessary to point out that these are also the components found in the Christian celebration of the Lord's Supper. We, too, have a sacrifice, the death of the Lamb of God. The blood of this sacrifice in the Communion wine is placed first upon the altar. There follows the proclamation of the word and our affirmation of commitment. The cup of the new covenant in Christ's blood is then given to the people. And by joining in the Communion meal, we believe we eat and drink with the Lord. Here, in this account of Exod. 24, then, we find a description of a covenant meal which reminds us immediately of the Lord's Supper.

The important point to see, however, is that the service laid upon Israel is not only his but ours. We, too, are called into the covenant community. In the context of the grace of God in Jesus Christ's life and death and resurrection, we are asked to make our decision. But if we decide to give our life to the Lord, to enter into the new covenant as members of his Church, we surrender our own wills and become responsible to God alone. No longer is our task to adjust to our world or to our society. Our mission is to become obedient to a will transcending them both. And our pledge is to live as faithful members of God's community of peace and love, the Church. We join hands with our fellow Christians in a common loyalty to God. All this is laid upon us if we partake of the Lord's Supper. For there at his table, we, like Israel, become his alone. It is the covenant with God which defines the nature of the service owed to him.

4. "TO YOUR DESCENDANTS I GIVE THIS LAND": THE CONQUEST OF CANAAN

(Read Joshua 1-11, 23-24)

That Israel did not keep the covenant made with Yahweh at Mount Sinai is evident if we read the accounts of Israel's time in the wilderness in Exod. 32-33 and Num. 10:11 ff. Even while still at the holy mountain, the people broke the

55

covenant commands by making for themselves a golden calf to worship in the place of Yahweh (Exod. 32), and though the Lord was constantly forgiving, Israel would not trust his guidance and provision. The people feared that they would die for lack of food and water in the desert (Num. 20-21). And when they heard the report of conditions in the promised land, they wanted to forget about their redemption and return to the land of Egypt (Num. 14:1-4). Even when God gave them the necessities of life, they bitterly complained that such necessities were not more delectable: "We remember the fish we ate in Egypt for nothing, the cucumbers, the melons, the leeks, the onions, and the garlic; but now our strength [appetite] is dried up, and there is nothing at all but this manna to look at" (Num. 11:5-6). It is little wonder that Ezek. 20 and Ps. 78 and 106 look back on the wilderness time as a period of utter rebellion on Israel's part. This people who were to serve the Lord did not surrender to him at all.

And yet, Yahweh's purpose to fulfill his promise cannot be overcome by man's sin. "My presence will go with you," he told them, "and I will give you rest." (Exod. 33:14). Despite their mutterings and complaints and fears, God led his own toward Canaan. According to priestly traditions in the book of Exodus, they lived from day to day by his hand (Exod. 16:9-30). Deuteronomy tells us he gave them clothing and prevented the sandals from wearing off their feet (29:5). And both Deuteronomy and Jeremiah emphasize the marvelous nature of Yahweh's care by picturing the desert as a land full of terrors and death (Deut. 8:15; Jer. 2:6). Through the wilderness of "'drought and deep darkness," God guided his son.

We now know that the actual conquest of Canaan was

probably neither a swift nor a united effort on the part of all of Israel under the leadership of Joshua. The account of the supposed subjugation of all of Canaan in Josh. 2-9 actually deals only with the conquest of the territory later allotted to the tribe of Benjamin. And Josh. 10 is an independent Ephraimite tale, with Joshua of the tribe of Ephraim, as its hero. These independent tribal legends have been placed within a framework, constructed by a later editor, in order to make it appear that all of Israel entered into the promised land, annihilated its Canaanite inhabitants, greatly expanded its borders, and settled down in the territory which was divided among the twelve tribes.

In truth, probably each tribe or group in Israel made its own conquest and settlement, without being united behind the one leader Joshua. The conquest was slow and gradual, with a raid here or a push there. Some Hebrews were already in the land before the conquest began, and all of the land was not taken until the time of David. Above all, the Canaanite inhabitants were not exterminated, a fact which is confirmed not only by Judg. 1, but also by the list of tribal borders in Joshua and by the fact that from this time on the Canaanite religion proved one of the strongest temptations to the members of Israel.

Nevertheless, by whatever manner, Israel settled in Canaan and formed an amphictyony, united in the worship of Yahweh. And every member of this religious unity came to consider Yahweh's gift of the land as a gift to him personally. God had brought his people into Canaan and fought on their behalf. He had given them their inheritance "flowing with milk and honey." By the time of David, they had "rest from all of their enemies round about them." In these events, each Israelite saw God's mercy extended to him.

More than this, Israel saw in the conquest of Canaan the fulfillment of God's promise to the patriarchs. Now all had been brought to completion. Yahweh had made Israel a great nation and brought them into a special relationship with himself, in the covenant. He had given them the land as he promised he would do. Looking back over this history from the time of the sixth century B.C., the editor of the Book of Joshua celebrated God's faithfulness:

Thus the Lord gave to Israel all the land which he swore to give to their fathers; and having taken possession of it, they settled there. And the Lord gave them rest on every side just as he had sworn to their fathers; not one of all their enemies had withstood them, for the Lord had given all their enemies into their hands. *Not one of all the good promises which the Lord had made to the house of Israel had failed; all came to pass.* (Josh. 21:43-45; cf. 23:14.)

God had promised and he had fulfilled. God had spoken and he had done it. Back there in Mesopotamia in about the eighteenth century B.C., God had called Abraham and revealed his purpose and word to him. And through eight centuries of difficulties and struggles, despite his people's mistrust and rebellion, God had worked and fought and forgiven in order to keep his word. Israel, the covenant nation, was settled into Canaan. The witness of the first six books of the Old Testament is that our Lord keeps his promise.

Strangely enough, however, one element has been forgotten in this witness—the promise to Abraham to make Israel the means of blessing for all nations. Apparently the editor of Joshua overlooked this part of the promise. But though some of the biblical writers forgot it, God never did. We shall later see it reappear as we continue Israel's story.

Chapter IV

The Relation of the Law to the Promise

1. ISRAEL'S UNDERSTANDING OF THE COVENANT COMMANDMENTS

(Read Deuteronomy)

It is perhaps obvious by now that the Old Testament is not a legalistic book. We have seen acting thus far through its story not a God of strict and impartial justice, but a God of faithfulness, of forgiveness, and of love. Indeed, we have found on its pages a record of the acts of the same God we know from the New Testament.

And yet, the book of the old covenant contains many laws, the majority of them being collected together in Exodus, Leviticus, Numbers, and Deuteronomy. All of these laws are reported to have been proclaimed by God to Israel through his prophet Moses at Mount Sinai or in the wilderness. And taken together, these laws were seen as the requirements which Yahweh laid upon Israel in the covenant relationship.

When the layman views this legal collection, which actually

is the product of many years and traditions, he cannot escape the feeling that Hebrew religion was legalistic and that Israel saw its relationship to Yahweh to be dependent upon keeping the law. Because this view of the Old Testament is so widespread, it is necessary to examine more closely the actual manner in which Israel understood the law. Did the Hebrews really believe they could have no fellowship with Yahweh unless they perfectly fulfilled his covenant commandments?

Clearly, and for several reasons, the answer is no. In the first place, as we have seen, it was Yahweh who initiated the relationship with his people. He it was who brought them up out of the land of Egypt and made them his own. He chose them to be the people of his own possession and entered into fellowship with them. It was not obedience to the law which established Israel's relation to the Lord, but the love and desire of that Lord to have Israel as his people and to use them for his universal purpose in the world. Until God rejected his chosen people, they were considered his. He had set up the relationship with them. He alone could abrogate it.

Again, when we study a summary of Yahweh's will such as is found in the Ten Commandments it becomes clear that this is no code for a legalistic life. If it were designed to be a law by which Israel established and maintained his relationship with Yahweh, it would have to deal with ever so many more details and areas of life. It would have to tell what should be done in every situation, as the teachings of the later scribes and Pharisees did. But it does not. It merely rules out that which is absolutely forbidden by Yahweh. It summarizes what a man must not do, but it says nothing about what a man should do. In short, it points out that which is forbidden to him who already stands in fellowship with God. It makes no attempt to give the rules by which that fellowship can be established.

In the third place, if breaking the law meant that Israel at the same time forfeited its relationship with Yahweh, then there could be no forgiveness in the Old Testament. Any breach of the law would automatically cut off the sinner from the Lord. But it does not. The law itself makes provision for the forgiveness of sin, and the high point of the whole priestly ritual is the Day of Atonement (Lev. 16), when the priests, on behalf of Yahweh, atone for the sins of the people. Yahweh does not cut off the sinner in Israel from his grace. Rather, he offers a means whereby that sin is forgiven and blotted out. Despite the fact that Israel breaks the law, Yahweh's mercy and fellowship with him prevail.

Fourth, it is clear in the Old Testament, just as in the New, that a man is considered righteous before God not through works but through faith. This could be illustrated from many passages, but two psalms will perhaps suffice to illumine the point. In Ps. 32, the author considers himself to be among the righteous and those who are upright in heart (vs. 11). And yet, the entire psalm deals with God's forgiveness of his sins! His righteousness consists not in the fact that he perfectly obeys the law, but in the fact that he confesses his guilt and trusts in the mercy of the Lord. This man throws himself completely on God and in God's eyes is justified. His faith, not his works, is that which makes him righteous before his Lord.

Similarly, in Ps. 69, we find the prayer of a man who is sick and falsely accused. He prays for God's deliverance and vengeance upon his enemies. Clearly he counts himself righteous as over against those who persecute him (vs. 28). But again he makes no claim to have perfectly obeyed the law.

"O God, thou knowest my folly," he prays, "the wrongs I have done are not hidden from thee" (vs. 5). And yet, he throws himself on God in utter dependence on God's action. He cries to God (vs. 1), he waits for God (vs. 3), he seeks him, he hopes in him (vs. 6). In short, he is a man of faith, and it is this faith which is his righteousness. "The Lord hears the needy," he rejoices (vs. 33). God saves those who have no other helper, but who completely trust in him.

When we read in Gen. 15:6, therefore, that Abraham trusts in God's promise and that this trust is counted as his righteousness, or in Hab. 2:4 that "the righteous shall live by his faith," we are encountering no isolated instances of justification by faith in the Old Testament. We are reading specific expressions of the major Old Testament view of the relationship with God, as Paul repeatedly points out. It is not obedience to the law which makes a man acceptable to the Lord, but the complete surrender of that man to his God in faith. This surrender, this faith, is the heart of the covenant demand, as we saw in Chapter III, and without such faith no works of the law can bring Israel into relationship with his Lord (cf. Matt. 19:16-22). It is Israel's faithful acceptance of his given status as a servant to the Lord which constitutes the nature of the divine-human relationship in most of the Old Testament. God has set up a fellowship with his people. Israel's task is simply to surrender to him.

Within this fellowship, this new life which God has provided, the law serves as a guide to the covenant people. As we have said, it defines the nature of Israel's service to the Lord. It is God's "teaching" or "instruction" for his people, as the Hebrew word for law, torah, indicates. It tells Israel how to act, the way to walk as the redeemed of Yahweh. The redemption has already taken place. The new life of the fellowship has already been established. Now the law acts as a guidepost along the way.

As a result, Israel never sees the law as a burden, but rather as one of Yahweh's greatest gifts. Having elected Israel and given him a new life, Yahweh now does not leave Israel alone to stumble in the dark, but he provides a teaching and a way. Of all the nations on the earth, Yahweh chooses to guide Israel, and Israel sees this as the best gift that Yahweh could have given him:

Behold, I have taught you statutes and ordinances, as the Lord my God commanded me, that you should do them in the land which you are entering to take possession of it. Keep them and do them; for that will be your wisdom and your understanding in the sight of the peoples, who, when they hear all these statutes, will say, "Surely this great nation is a wise and understanding people." For what great nation is there that has a god so near to it as the Lord our God is to us, whenever we call upon him? And what great nation is there, that has statutes and ordinances so righteous as all this law which I set before you this day? (Deut. 4:5-8.)

The law is a gift which shows Yahweh's special grace to Israel. Therefore, Israel loves the law and delights in it (Ps. 40:8). It is his meditation day and night (Ps. 1:2), a gift more to be desired than gold and sweeter than honey (Ps. 19:10). Israel praises Yahweh for his law (Ps. 19:8 ff.) and thanks him for his commandments (Ps. 119).

We must not interpret all of this to mean, however, that the Israelite is not expected to obey the law. He is. Obedience to the law does not make him righteous before God and it does not establish his fellowship with the Lord. And yet, in neither Old Testament nor New is there any thought that obedience to God's commandments is a matter of indifference. The classic statement of the covenant relationship in the Old Testament contains a condition: "Now therefore, *if* you will obey my voice and keep my covenant, you shall be my own possession among all peoples." (Exod. 19:5). And Jesus repeatedly emphasizes the necessity of obedience:

> If you would enter life, keep the commandments. (Matt. 19:17.)
> If you love me, you will keep my commandments. (John 14:15.)
> If you keep my commandments, you will abide in my love, just as I have kept my Father's commandments and abide in his love. (John 15:10.)

The biblical relationship with God brings with it commandments, and the church is expected to obey these commandments for two reasons. The first concerns faith in God's lordship; the second, our response to God's love.

To enter into covenant relationship with God means to accept him as the Lord of one's life, as we have seen. It means that one becomes responsive to a divine will lying outside one's own being and one's own circumstances and culture and environment. Therefore, when we become members of the Christian church, we do so by acknowledging that Jesus Christ is our Lord. This was probably the earliest form of confession in the New Testament church: Jesus is Lord.

We make this confession; we accept God as the Lord of our lives only by faith. In faith, we acknowledge that God has acted in the past, in a holy history. In faith, we confess that God is ruling over our present lives. In faith, we affirm that he will continue to lead us and to guide the course of all history, until he finally establishes his kingdom among all men. In short, by faith we give over our lives to the action and rule of God. We trust that he has acted, that he can act, and that he will act in the future. And faith becomes essentially that attitude whereby we give God room to act, whereby we turn the course of our lives and our history over to him. Faith is the fulfillment of our covenant relationship with God. Our faith is our righteousness.

But in every part of the Bible, such faith issues in obedience to the revealed will of God, because we cannot confess Yahweh as the Lord of our lives and at the same time, ignore his gracious guiding of our lives. The man of faith obeys the law, not because it sets up his relationship with God and not because he becomes righteous through the law, but because such obedience is a manifestation of his faith, because such obedience affirms that Yahweh is, in truth, Lord of his life and therefore he takes Yahweh's will for his life seriously.

For this reason, the epistle of James says that faith without works is dead. For this reason, Paul's letters abound with ethical admonitions. For this reason, Jesus proclaims a new law on the shores of Galilee. For this reason, the prophets condemn Israel for not following the law. And for this reason, obedience to the law is expected in the Old Testament. Faith in the Lordship of Yahweh issues in obedience, because faith gives itself to be led by Yahweh, and because it is through his law that Yahweh does indeed lead.

In the light of all of this, the true import of the doctrine of justification by faith comes clear. It can hardly mean that the actions of a man are indifferent. That would be to pervert the entire biblical understanding of faith. For in the Bible faith is never separated from a man's works. Faith is righteousness before God, faith fulfills the covenant demand of God for surrender to his absolute lordship, but faith issues in obedience to the will of that God whom we acknowledge as our Lord.

There is in the Old Testament, however, another reason why Israel is expected to obey the law, and this is illumined most clearly in the book of Deuteronomy.

Deuteronomy[1] is written in the form of a farewell sermon of Moses to Israel in the land of Moab, shortly before Moses' death. In the picture our authors have given us, Israel stands before the promised land. He has not yet entered into his rest and inheritance. Actually, we know that the book dates from the seventh century B.C. and that it is addressed to the southern kingdom of Judah. The northern kingdom has fallen, the monarchy has long ago replaced the old amphictyony, Assyria has laid waste Judah under Hezekiah, and Manasseh has perverted the Yahweh cult with every kind of Canaanite syncretism, including human sacrifice and the persecution of the prophets and their followers.

Deuteronomy therefore questions if Israel is still the chosen people of Yahweh. After the six centuries of sin and apostasy which have separated the Israel of the seventh century from the original Israel at Sinai, after all that has taken place under the monarchy in Judah, is Israel still the people of God? He is admittedly an evil people (Deut. 9:6, 13; 31:27). Do the election and covenant still stand, therefore, or has the sin of Israel abrogated his relationship with the Lord?

The answer of Deuteronomy is unhesitating. "This day," it proclaims to Judah, "you have become the people of the Lord your God" (Deut. 27:9). Despite all that they have

[1] We are indebted at many points in our discussion of Deuteronomy to G. von Rad, *Theologie des Alten Testaments*, Vol. I, Chr. Kaiser Verlag Muenchen, 1957.

done to disobey the covenant commands, despite all of their apostasy and sin, the Israelites are still a people holy to Yahweh, a people for his own possession, out of all the peoples on the face of the earth (Deut. 7:6; 14:2, 21; 26:18-19).

Yahweh has loved Israel with a great love, not out of any merit on Israel's part, but out of his free grace and mercy (Deut. 7:6-8). Though heaven and earth belong to the Lord, he has drawn near to Israel in the fathers and loved them and promised them and their descendants the land of Canaan (Deut. 6:10; 7:8; 10:14-15). In the law of Deuteronomy, the author believes that Yahweh now gives Israel the full revelation of his will (Deut. 4:2). Corresponding to this one will, he will give Israel one cult site, the temple in Jerusalem, where he will lay his name and receive Israel's worship (Deut. 12:2-14).

More than this, Yahweh will give Israel a good land, richly watered, full of fruits and vineyards and rich in mineral treasures (Deut. 8:7-9). It will have great cities and beautiful houses which will be ready and waiting for the Israelites (Deut. 6:10-11). And it will enjoy Yahweh's special care, since he will never take his eyes off of it (Deut. 11:10-12). Indeed, Yahweh will give to Israel a material, earthly paradise, which will be sufficient for all of his needs (Deut. 28:1-14). Coupled with this, Israel will have rest from all his enemies round about him (Deut. 12:9-10; 25:19), and he will enjoy a secure and peaceful existence in the land of promise. Such are the gifts which the seventh-century authors of Deuteronomy see Yahweh to have given his people across the years. In many respects, this book is in the Old Testament truly *the* book of the love of God.

If God has loved Israel so much, however, then the one

response appropriate on Israel's part is to love God in return. Mindful of all the blessings which the Lord has bestowed upon him, Israel is to love God by cherishing his word and walking in its way, constantly, through every day of his life in the promised land. In short, the proper response of Israel to God's care is loving obedience to his will, which is revealed in his law. This is expressed in the central passage of Deuteronomy, the Shema', which is still recited today in Jewish synagogues around the world:

Hear, O Israel: The Lord our God is one Lord; and you shall love the Lord your God with all your heart, and with all your soul, and with all your might. And these words which I command you this day shall be upon your heart; and you shall teach them diligently to your children, and shall talk of them when you sit in your house, and when you walk by the way, and when you lie down, and when you rise. And you shall bind them as a sign upon your hand, and they shall be as frontlets between your eyes. And you shall write them on the doorposts of your house and on your gates. (Deut. 6:4-9.)

Here in Deuteronomy we see the second reason why obedience to the law is expected of Israel in the Old Testament. Yahweh has loved him with a love which is completely unmerited on his part, and Israel's only proper response to such love is thankfulness and gratitude and loving obedience to the will of Yahweh in return.

Put into the language of our own faith, it means we cannot turn our back on a God who loves us so much that he is willing to die for us. We cannot slap him in the face and refuse to listen to his word of guidance, given in his commandments. His love prompts our obedient love in return. And the motive of that obedience is a heartfelt willingness to do all for the God who has done all for us.

For this reason, the commandment to love God is in Deuteronomy and in the teachings of Jesus the first and greatest commandment. It is found twelve times in the book of Deuteronomy and it is made the basis of all other commands. For if a man truly loves the Lord, he will willingly follow his guidance.

As in the New Testament, however, the authors of Deuteronomy are zealous to lay the foundation for love. There is constant emphasis on the deeds of Yahweh in the past and on his acts of loving mercy toward Israel. Similarly, Deuteronomy is concerned that these acts not be forgotten. For if God's community fails to remember God's love, which has been manifested through his concrete deeds in history, then there will be no basis laid in its life for its responding obedience and love. In many respects, faith is, in the Bible, founded on the memory of God's acts in history.

Deuteronomy therefore urges upon its readers the religious education of their children. The children are to be told of what Yahweh has done—which is the true nature of religious education—and sacred traditions are to be passed down from one generation to the next. Moreover, each new generation is to be brought so vividly into remembrance of the past that the covenant made with Israel at Sinai becomes a covenant made with them in the present: "The Lord our God made a covenant with us in Horeb [Sinai]. Not with our fathers did the Lord make this covenant, but with us, who are all of us here alive this day." (Deut. 5:2-3; cf. 29:10-15.)

Further, Deuteronomy is concerned that its readers understand their religion. Perhaps no book in the Old Testament makes more appeal to the hearts and minds of its hearers than does this one. All is simplified within it. No problem defies solution. Only that which is plausible to the layman is treated. All can be grasped, and none of the commands is incapable of fulfillment:

For this commandment which I command you this day is not too hard for you, neither is it far off. It is not in heaven, that you should say, "Who will go up for us to heaven, and bring it to us, that we may hear it and do it?" Neither is it beyond the sea, that you should say, "Who will go over the sea for us, and bring it to us, that we may hear it and do it?" But the word is very near you; it is in your mouth and in your heart, so that you can do it. (Deut. 30:11-14.)

These words do not come from a legalistic book. There is no striving and seeking here to win one's own salvation. Obedience to the letter of the law is not required to set up the relationship with God. The relationship has already been established by Yahweh, who has loved Israel with a great love. Now Israel is called to respond to that love with an obedience commensurate with it. His response is one of loving willingness and gratitude, and from it all else follows.

"You shall love the Lord your God with all your heart, and with all your soul, and with all your mind. This is the great and first commandment." (Matt. 22:37-38.)

2. THE TRANSFORMATION OF THE UNDERSTANDING OF THE LAW IN JUDAISM

(Read Ezra 7-8, Nehemiah 8, Ezra 9-10, Nehemiah 9-10)

In view of the fact that Jesus apparently took over and used in his teachings Deuteronomy's understanding of the law as based on love, the layman could well question why it was, then, that Jesus came so violently into conflict with the teachers and practitioners of the law, the scribes and Pharisees. This question has many ramifications, but we can perhaps best answer it by showing how post-exilic Judaism, that is, the religion of the Hebrews from the time of Ezra on, transformed Deuteronomy's understanding of God's commandments.

As we have seen, initially the law was made necessary by the presence of God with his people Israel. When they were plucked out of bondage to their historical circumstances in Egypt and set in the wilderness in the "glorious liberty of the children of God," they were together brought into relationship with a Lord towards whom they had no idea how to act. The law was given as a guide. It defined Israel's action and the nature of the service he was to render to his Lord. But the law had meaning only because it was given in the context of the election. It was necessary only because it defined the manner of Israel's action within the fellowship which God had established. Had Yahweh not entered into relationship with his people, there would have been no need for the law. Had he not been able to declare, "I am the Lord your God, who brought you out of the land of Egypt, out of the house of bondage," there would have been no reason for continuing, "You shall have no other gods before me" (Exod. 20:2-3; Deut. 5:6-7). The law assumed that God was with his people. And it was this presence of Yahweh with Israel which made them distinct from all other peoples on the face of the earth (Exod. 33:16). "Israel" was synonymous with a "visited" folk. Israel was those with whom Yahweh elected to dwell.

The presence of Yahweh in Israel was, through the first

seven centuries of Israel's history, visibly and materially demonstrated in several ways. In the priestly traditions, it is remembered that he descended in the fiery light of his glory to the tabernacle at Sinai and in the wilderness (Exod. 40: 34-38), making known his will to Moses. Other ancient beliefs connected his presence with the ark, on which he was invisibly enthroned (I Sam. 4:4; II Kings 19:15). This ark not only accompanied the Israelites on their wilderness wanderings (Num. 10:35-36; 14:38-45), but during the conquest (Josh. 3-6), coming finally to rest in the temple of Solomon, the dwelling place of the Lord (I Kings 8). Here in the temple of Jerusalem, Yahweh caused his name to dwell (Deut. 12:5), another way of saying that this was where he was present. Through the temple and its cult, in short, Yahweh was made manifest to his people.

Yahweh's presence with Israel was also demonstrated by his gift of the land, and the fact that Israel dwelt in Palestine was material evidence of Yahweh's nearness. Only because the Lord had entered into relationship with Israel did that people possess the fields and hills and towns that were theirs.

Finally, as we shall see in the next chapter, Yahweh's presence with Israel was manifested in the fact that the house of David ruled over Judah. Yahweh had entered into relationship with his people through the means of an eternal covenant with David. As long as a descendant of David sat on the throne, the people could be sure that God was with them.

In short, Israel knew God was with him, because he experienced the actions of God in his history and the presence of God in his cult. And "Israel" was all those people who entered into this experience. They were those who worshiped in the temple which housed the ark and who praised God's name and

73

glory. They were those who lived in the promised land that had been given them and who were subject to the Davidic ruler. They were all those who, through faith or family or patriotism were brought somehow into connection with the historical results of the actions of God. They were the "visited" people, the people who had been met by God and who enjoyed the results of his actions. Because God was with them, they needed the law.

It is somewhat startling to realize, therefore, that the external results of this entire history of Israel with God was wiped out by the Babylonian exile of 587 B.C. The temple of Jerusalem, with its ark of the covenant, was destroyed, along with the royal city. The Davidic ruler was deposed, blinded, imprisoned, and his sons murdered. The entire land of Judah was laid waste, and all but its poorest peasants were carried into captivity. In one great holocaust, Israel's history with Yahweh was no longer visible upon the face of the earth. There was no land, no king, no temple, no cult. It was as if Yahweh had never acted. Israel no longer had any sign that God had entered into relationship with him. Israel had no concrete manifestation that the election had ever taken place—none, that is, except one. Israel still had the law!

Here was the one element which the Babylonians could not destroy. Here was the one manifestation of God's action which could be carried into exile and back again to Palestine. Here was the one proof that God had chosen Israel—Israel was the people who had God's law!

When Nehemiah and Ezra returned to Palestine with groups of exiles in the fifth century B.C. in order politically and religiously to reconstitute the Jewish community, under the sovereignty of the Persian empire, they found a diverse mixture of peoples living in the tiny subprovince of Judah (Neh. 13:23 ff., Ezra 9:1 ff). Jews had intermarried with Canaanites and Moabites, Egyptians and Amorites. Some even spoke foreign tongues. And the question confronting Nehemiah, but also especially Ezra, who was to reorder the religious life of the community (Ezra 7:12-26), was, who among this mixed multitude were the elected people of Yahweh? Who truly belonged to Israel as his visited people? Who were really members of the chosen race?

There was only one measure by which to judge. The true members of Israel were those who followed the law, because the law was the last remaining evidence on earth that the election had ever taken place. If a man was not obedient to the law of God, he could not be among the chosen. From the time of Ezra onward, membership in the community of Israel was determined by adherence to the commandments.

In other words, the understanding of the place of the law in Israelite life was now completely transformed, and essentially the law took the place of the election. No longer was membership in Israel a gift of God, given by his gracious acts in history. No longer was the Israelite one who had been redeemed from Egypt or settled in the promised land or born into a nation ruled by the Davidic king. No longer was it God's initiative which made the Israelite a member of the chosen race. Now each Hebrew had to earn his place in Israel by following the law. Now every Jew had to prove that he was elected by obeying the commandments. The law was no longer a guide within a community already established by God. It became the factor which constituted that community. And the necessity of the law was no longer based on the fact that God had set up a relationship with his people. The law itself

75

became the condition of that relationship. Only as a man obeyed the law did he become a member of Israel. Only as he was faithful to the commandments was he assured that he had been met by God and that God would continue to be with him.

We can see illustrated the nature of this transformation in the understanding of the law if we compare the understanding of Israel's worship in the Pentateuch with that found in the fourth century B.C. Books of Chronicles. Throughout the Pentateuch, that is, throughout the first five books of the Old Testament, everything that is done in Israel's worship is considered to be done "for Yahweh." There is nothing here akin to the modern-day search for a "worship experience." The subjective feelings of the worshiping congregation are of little importance, and while the individual Israelite undoubtedly often was touched emotionally in his worship, as the Psalms attest, the important element was not the arousal of the emotions but the service of God. Indeed, the Hebrew word for cult means "service." Everything was done "for Yahweh."

The great pilgrimage feasts were to be held for him (Lev. 23:41), as was the Passover (Exod. 12:11). The sabbath was for Yahweh (Exod. 16:23), as was the sacrifice (Lev. 1:2). Anything used in the worship service was set apart as holy to God, dedicated exclusively for his use and purpose.

But all this implied that God would be present with his people, and the highest point of Israelite worship was when Yahweh descended to the sacrifice. The officiating priest prepared the people for this descent with the cry, "Be still before the Lord" (cf. Zeph. 1:7; Zech. 2:13), and then Yahweh, the rider on the clouds, the Lord of glory, came to be with his community!

There was no thought that the rules and laws governing worship were necessary *in order that* Yahweh would be with his people. They were necessary because God would in fact be with them. Everything had to be done decently and in order because Yahweh would be present at the worship service. His presence with his people was the fact which made the ritual law necessary. The law was followed in order that Israel might conduct itself worthily before its Lord.

In the Books of Chronicles, however, this situation is exactly reversed. Now the cultic laws are necessary not *because* Yahweh is with his people. They are necessary *in order that* Yahweh will be with his people. We can see this in II Chron. 13:4-12, which in many ways is a synopsis of the thought of the Chronicler. Here King Abijah of Judah taunts the hated residents of the northern kingdom—a reflection of post-exilic Judah's controversy with the northern Samaritans. And the point of his taunt is that Yahweh is with Judah and not with the northern kingdom of Israel, because Judah has a legitimate priesthood, descended from Aaron, which makes the proper sacrifices and cares for the temple and its holy objects in the manner prescribed by the law. Only as the law is obeyed is Yahweh's presence guaranteed. It is a man's works which make him a member of the chosen people, a member of the community with which Yahweh chooses to dwell.

In Jesus' day, then, scribes and Pharisees could consider that they were God's elect, because they followed the law, while tax collectors and sinners had no place in the community because they broke the legal requirements. Against this legalism Jesus preached and acted, drawing upon Deuteronomy and the original Old Testament understanding of God's love toward Israel. Israel, Jesus affirmed, was not made

77

up of those who tried to earn their own election, but those who stood once more helpless in the wilderness of their own sin and circumstance and heard God's gracious words, "This day you have become the people of the Lord your God."

In truth, it is this message of the incredible mercy of God which forms the heart of the New Testament good news, that we are redeemed and chosen by God through the cross of Christ to be his people, his elect, despite anything that we have done or left undone. The only response possible, then, is that we love this God of the Bible with all of our hearts and souls and minds, that we lovingly follow his commandments because he has first loved us.

3. JESUS CHRIST AS A PROPHET LIKE MOSES

We cannot conclude this chapter on the law without saying a few words about Israel's supreme lawgiver, Moses, for this, too, will help us understand who Jesus Christ is.

In the New Testament, people frequently call Jesus a prophet, and we have at least two traditions in which he applies the term to himself: "A prophet is not without honor, except in his own country" (Mark 6:4). "It cannot be that a prophet should perish away from Jerusalem." (Luke 13:33.)

However, in Acts 3:22 and 7:37, we learn that the Jews of New Testament times were expecting God to raise up for them a very special kind of prophet, a prophet like Moses. In the Gospel according to John, we find this expectation clearly portrayed. "Are you the prophet?" the people inquire of John the Baptist (1:21, 25). But then, after Jesus feeds the five thousand, some of the people say, "This is indeed the prophet who is to come into the world" (John 6:14; cf. 7:40).

This New Testament expectation of a special prophet is

based on a promise from Deut. 18:15 ff. Here Moses tells the Israelites, "The Lord your God will raise up for you a prophet like me from among you, from your brethren—him you shall heed." From the time of Deuteronomy onward, the Israelites looked for this prophet. And some of them thought that they had found him in Jesus of Nazareth. What was there about our Lord which reminded them of Moses?

From all of the diverse and mixed traditions which we have concerning Moses in the Old Testament, we can only begin to guess the answer, and yet there are elements in the Mosaic tradition which we should especially notice.

Perhaps most noteworthy is the close relationship of Moses to the Lord. It is the function of the prophet in the Old Testament to speak God's word, to proclaim the message which God puts into his mouth (Exod. 4:10-16), to be the instrument whereby God releases into history his active and effective word of power. All of the prophets of the Old Testament are given means of communication with God which seem to go beyond those granted to ordinary men. As Jeremiah puts it, they have "stood in the council of the Lord to perceive and to hear his word" (Jer. 23:18).

And yet, Moses' fellowship with God goes beyond that granted to all other prophets.

If there is a prophet among you, I the Lord make myself known to him in a vision, I speak with him in a dream. Not so with my servant Moses; he is entrusted with all my house. With him I speak mouth to mouth, clearly, and not in dark speech; and he beholds the form of the Lord. (Num. 12:6-7.)

Thus, it is Moses who goes alone up Sinai to receive the law (Exod. 24:15-18), who speaks with the Lord on the mountain, and for whom Yahweh writes down his commandments (Deut. 5:22-27). Indeed, in Deuteronomy, it is through Moses alone that God speaks to his people. Elsewhere, Moses is so drawn into the realm of Yahweh that when he descends the mountain, his face still shines with the reflection of the glory of God (Exod. 34:29-35), and it is to this tradition that Paul directly refers in II Cor. 3-4, when he writes that we have been given "the light of the knowledge of the glory of God in the face of Christ" (II Cor. 4:6). The one who becomes a prophet like Moses shares Moses' intimate relation with the Lord.

Like other prophets of the Old Testament, Moses makes intercession for his people before God. He seeks God's judgment in their legal decisions (Exod. 18:19). He prays to God to heal their diseases (Num. 12:13). But most important, he intercedes for them in order that God will forgive their sins (Exod. 32:11-14). In fact, so concerned is Moses with the life and well-being of his people that he is willing to bear God's full judgment upon their sins in his own person (Exod. 32:32).

This means, in short, that Moses is a suffering mediator for Israel. When the people make the golden calf at the foot of mount Sinai, it is Moses who bears the wrath of the Lord for their sake, lying prostrate before the Lord forty days and forty nights, without food or water, praying and pleading with God that he destroy not his own (Deut. 9:16-29). And although Israel sins against God in the wilderness, it is Moses who bears their punishment, dying outside the promised land in order that Israel may enter into it (Deut. 1:37; 4:21-22). It is not hard to find parallels here with the New Testament message that Jesus Christ suffered for our sins.

But like the One who was to come after him, Moses bore

his role gladly, suffering for his people silently and without protest. It is said in Num. 12:3 that "the man Moses was very meek, more than all men that were on the face of the earth." In Deut. 3:24 and 34:5, Moses is called the servant of the Lord (cf. Rev. 15:3), and truly, the picture we have of him reminds one of Deutero-Isaiah's Suffering Servant:

> He was oppressed, and he was afflicted,
>   yet he opened not his mouth;
> like a lamb that is led to the slaughter,
>   and like a sheep that before its shearers is dumb,
>   so he opened not his mouth.
>
> .   .   .   .
>
> he was cut off out of the land of the living,
>   stricken for the transgression of my people?
>   (Isa. 53:7-8.)

We clearly see this total picture of Moses mirrored in Jesus of Nazareth. He, perfectly, was the Servant of the Lord, interceding and dying on behalf of his own that they might enter God's promised land. He, fully, was the long-awaited prophet, speaking God's word for him. He, truly, was the expected one like Moses. We should only note, as we conclude this section on the law that Deuteronomy states, "Him you shall heed" (Deut. 18:15).

Chapter V

A New Addition to the Promise:
The Establishment of
the Kingship in Israel

1. ISRAEL'S LIFE AS AN AMPHICTYONY: THE PERIOD OF THE JUDGES

(Read Judges 2:6-21:25; I Samuel 1-12)

Inevitably the church must come to terms with history. By the nature of its creation, the church is a separated people. It is a group of rebels against God, like the rest of mankind, who for no merit on their part and for no reason apparent to the rest of humanity are redeemed by God, given a new life, and drawn together in a community subject to God's Lordship and commandments. The church is separated from all other groups on earth and made servant to God alone. Its life is one of lonely uniqueness, apart from the rest of human history.

And yet, the church lives within history. The commandments which it is given to obey are to be followed not only in the separated sphere of the church's life, but also in relationship to those round about the church. And the mission which it is given to accomplish is one which involves the rest of the world. The church must inevitably learn to live with its nonchurch neighbors, while yet preserving the uniqueness of its own life. The church must, in short, learn to be in the world and yet not of it.

This was the problem which faced the people of the old covenant, Israel, and it was with the solution to this problem that Israel wrestled throughout its life. Yet perhaps the problem was most acute during Israel's time as an amphictyony, from about 1220 to 1020 B.C.

When Israel first settled into the promised land, he was surrounded on all sides by foreign peoples and religions. His constant fight was not only to resist the incursion of heathen belief and culture into his faith and practice, but also to protect himself from annihilation by surrounding peoples, seeking his land and goods. This fight makes up the story of the Book of Judges, and although a later editor has subjected this book to a somewhat stereotyped religious framework, we can gain something of an impression from it of Israel's early life as a settled people.

As we have mentioned earlier, Israel was united in a twelve tribe amphictyony in this period by a common worship and a common memory (see Chapter I). But the Israelites also occasionally came together in this time in a common military venture to fight against any enemy threatening the life of one of the twelve tribes.

These wars, as they were conducted by the Israelites, give the appearance of complete lack of any military organization. The Israelite army was made up of farmers, summoned hastily together to do battle. The leader of the army was one of their number, who was held to have received a special inspiration from God. And at no time could this leader, or Judge as he is called in the Old Testament, count on the co-operation of all the tribes of Israel. This can be seen very clearly in the Song of Deborah in Judges 5, where some of the tribes are rebuked for not joining in the war with the Canaanite Sisera (cf. vss. 16-17).

Actually, however, the Israelite cause was not as hopeless as it might seem from a military point of view. We now know that members of the Hebrew army were consecrated and prepared for their fight by the most careful religious and dedicatory rites. And the morale and might of the amphictyonic army were strengthened by the conviction that it had at its head an unconquerable man of war—Yahweh. Indeed, these wars which Israel fought in its early period were not considered to be Israel's struggles, but Yahweh's (Judg. 5:31). He it was who went out before his troops (Judg. 4:14), and he it was who gained the victory, fighting in the battle with supernatural means (Judg. 4:15; 7:22). Thus, in the story of Gideon, in Judges 7, Gideon is ordered to reduce the number of his troops, in order that the greatness of Yahweh's victory may be magnified, and when the Israelites plunge into the fray, their battle cry is, "A sword for the Lord and for Gideon" (7:20)! Such fervor and dedication often met with success on the field of battle.

And yet, it was a limited success at best. We read in Judges 21:25, "In those days there was no king in Israel; every man did what was right in his own eyes" (cf. 18:1), a somewhat rueful admission on the part of the editor of the Book of Judges that the twelve-tribe amphictyony was by no means a unified whole. In times of crisis, only a few of the tribes responded to the call to war. The Judge who arose to lead them had no official status, and he was unknown outside his own tribe, sometimes unknown within it. There was an inconstancy and uncertainty of leadership which made unified action impossible. The amphictyonic organization was simply too weak to meet the threats to Israel's existence.

Threats there were indeed. Israel lived in the international corridor of the world, the buffer of the great empires. Moreover, the tribal territories were so situated that the Israelites faced constant raids into their lands. The tribes of Reuben and Gad bordered on Moab and Ammon, and in the eleventh century B.C., Moab took over Reuben's territory, whereupon the latter disappeared from history. The western half of the tribe of Manasseh had its northern border fringed with the fortified cities of the Canaanites. But most threatening of all, the territory of the promised land was invaded by the sea people of Crete.

We know that shortly after 1200 B.C., a large group of peoples from the islands of Greece attempted to invade Egypt, but were defeated by Rameses III about 1175 B.C. and pushed back into Canaan. Among these peoples were the Philistines, from whom we derive the name "Palestine." These people settled along Palestine's coastal plain, with five principle cities at Gaza, Ashkelon, Ashdod, Ekron and Gath. Each city, with the area it controlled, was ruled by a "lord," who, though independent, co-operated with the others in important matters. The Philistines therefore were able to act as a united political and military group, and it was they who constituted the most serious threat to Israel's existence in the amphictyonic period. They devastated the central sanctuary of Israel at Shiloh (cf. Jer. 7:12-14; 26:6), and they pushed as far inland as the city of Beth-shan, near the western banks of the Jordan (cf. I Sam. 31:10). In fact, between 1050 and 1020 B.C., they were able for the most part to dominate Israel politically. Toward the end of the eleventh century B.C., Israel faced the real possibility of annihilation.

In this situation, Israel had to come to terms with the problems of history. He had to have a leader capable of unifying tribal action and policy. He had now settled down in a land, as a nation among other nations, and that historical situation demanded a central control. Israel, facing the threat of the Philistines, had to have a king! "We will have a king over us, that we also may be like all the nations, and that our king may govern us and go out before us and fight our battles." (I Sam. 8:19-20; cf. vs. 5.) Such was the nature of the demand which the Israelites laid upon their last Judge, Samuel.

The truth of the matter is˗that Israel already had a king. Yahweh was his king, and from the time of the Exodus on, Yahweh had ruled over his people (cf. Exod. 15:18), enthroned upon the ark, leading them in battle, conquering all their foes (cf. I Sam. 12:7-12). The Judge Gideon therefore had refused to become a king over Israel. "I will not rule over you," he had told the people, "and my son will not rule over you; the Lord will rule over you" (Judg. 8:23). And Abimelech's abortive attempt to rule the inhabitants of Shechem brought his own downfall (Judg. 9). To trust the leadership and protection of someone other than Yahweh was to exhibit a lack of faith, and by demanding that Samuel anoint for them a king, the Israelites were rejecting the sovereignty of Yahweh. "They have not rejected you," God told Samuel, "but they have rejected me from being king over them" (I Sam. 8:7). The prophet Hosea was later to

86

castigate Israel's demand for a king as an act of apostasy (Hos. 8:4; 13:10-11).

And yet, the Philistines were settled on the coastal plain, and Israel was threatened with annihilation. His dilemma was little different from that of the modern-day Christian who knows an enemy to be lurking behind an iron curtain. Should we seek human means to defend ourselves, and thereby perhaps at least preserve the church alive, or should we trust all to the defense of God, believing that he will give us victory? What will be the cost in innocent suffering and what is our responsibility to the world? What is the one course clearly demanded by faith, and which is true service of the Lord? The Israelites could answer these questions with no more common consensus than can we. They were faced with the church's contradictory task of being in the world but not of it.

The reality of this contradiction in Israel's life is exhibited by the fact that in the book of I Samuel, there are other passages (I Sam. 9:1-10:16; 11) which view the kingship, not as an act of rebellion against Yahweh's rule, but as a gracious gift on Yahweh's part. In this strand of tradition, the Lord takes the initiative in anointing a king to rule Israel:

Now the day before Saul came, the Lord had revealed to Samuel: "Tomorrow about this time I will send to you a man from the land of Benjamin, and you shall anoint him to be a prince over my people Israel. He shall save my people from the hand of the Philistines; for I have seen the affliction of my people, because their cry has come to me." (I Sam. 9:15-16.)

Just as the Lord had heard the cry of his people from Egypt and delivered them out of bondage, so here he heeds their plea for defense against the Philistines and makes provision for a ruler to deliver them from their enemy.

It seems doubtful that the Christian reader of the Old Testament can choose between these contradictory views of the kingship in I Samuel, for neither one holds within itself the full truth. Israel was faced with a situation in which he had to have a king, and Yahweh graciously provided for the needs of his people. And yet, to need any other than God is somehow to belittle his all-sufficiency and to turn aside to trust in other supports and rulers. That the Old Testament presents to us both sides of the truth is testimony to its realism and to its understanding of the struggles of faith within history.

2. ISRAEL'S FIRST KING: THE TRAGEDY OF SAUL

(Read I Samuel 13–II Samuel 1)

It was Saul of Benjamin to whom there fell the unhappy task of being king over a people whose real king was Yahweh, and the contradictions inherent in this task proved too much for the first Israelite monarch. To make matters worse, Saul was not at all suited to be a king. He was much too tall (I Sam. 9:2; 10:23), much too nervous and shy, much too easily moved. When the lot indicated that he was chosen for the office, he hid himself among the tribal baggage (I Sam. 10:22). When an enemy showed him a kindness, he broke into tears (I Sam. 24:16). Israel's first monarch was a neurotic, and his office made him a tragic neurotic.

Although Saul fulfilled his people's expectations by leading them victoriously in battle against the Philistines and other enemies (I Sam. 14:47-48), he found it impossible also perfectly to serve God. The insuperable nature of his task is well illustrated by one of the two stories which we have of the rejection of Saul, in I Sam. 13:2-15. Saul had called out his people to Gilgal to fight against the Philistines. But before entering the battle, it was the religious practice for a priest to offer a sacrifice to the Lord. Samuel was expected to do so, but for seven days he made no appearance. Saul's troops were demoralized in the interval, many of them returning to their homes. In desperation, Saul himself offered the sacrifice, taking upon himself Samuel's prerogatives, despite the fact that such an act was a transgression of the cultic law. There seemed no other way to gain victory over the enemy than by this disobedience to the commandment of God.

The result of Saul's disobedience was that the kingdom was taken away from him and the Spirit of God, enabling him to rule, was given to the youngest son of Jesse, David, from the Judean city of Bethlehem (I Sam. 13:14; 15:28; 16:13-14). Saul's downfall was occasioned by the fact that absolute obedience to Yahweh often allows no compromise before the necessities of history. For, as in the other account of the rejection, in I Sam. 15, to compromise is to exhibit a basic lack of trust in God's guidance. Saul could not be a successful ruler of a people whose real ruler was Yahweh.

The rest of the story of Saul is unrelieved tragedy. It is clear that David and not Saul is the king after Yahweh's own heart (I Sam. 13:14), and every step upward for David means a step downward for the rejected Saul. David is more successful in battle (I Sam. 18:7), and the people transfer their esteem to him (I Sam. 18:28, 30). Saul's daughter Michal falls in love with David (I Sam. 18:20) and becomes his wife (I Sam. 18:27), despite all of Saul's efforts to prevent a union which will mean that David will share in the power of the royal house. Even Saul's son is drawn so to David that he makes a covenant with him, loving David as one of his flesh and giving him his valuables (I Sam. 18). The picture we have is of a Saul divested of all support and love. He is forced to go on acting as a king, though every step takes him closer to his doom. Of all of the characterizations in the Old Testament, that of Saul is the nearest to Greek tragedy. It is the very role of greatness which is given to him that makes his downfall inevitable, but play out that role he must until the grievous end.

Traditions never gathered about the figure of Saul as they did about David. He never became a type or norm for anything in Israel, and some parts of the Old Testament brush him off (I Chron. 10:13-14) or ignore him completely (Ps. 78). And yet, when we read of his final days in I Samuel 28 and of his courage in the face of certain death in I Samuel 31, we cannot help feeling that David's lament for Saul was appropriate:

> Thy glory, O Israel, is slain upon thy high places!
> How are the mighty fallen! (II Sam. 1:19)

3. THE RISE AND REIGN OF DAVID

(Read II Samuel 2–I Kings 2)

The reader is vividly aware throughout the story of Saul of the activity of Israel's God. It is Saul's relationship to Yahweh which determines the course of his life. It is his disobedience of Yahweh which brings doom upon his head. But the same cannot be said of the account of Saul's successor, David. Despite the fact that we are told at the beginning of David's story that he is the chosen Messiah, i.e. anointed, of Yahweh and that he is the bearer of the Spirit of God,

Yahweh seems often curiously absent from the history of Israel's greatest king.

Certainly this is true of David's rise to power. Everything that he does is politically correct, seemingly calculated, and cunningly designed to place him on Israel's throne. And although it is made clear that the Lord is with David (II Sam. 5:10), the reader cannot help feeling that it is largely David's ambition and sagacity which account for his success.

First of all, there is David's lament at the death of Saul and Jonathan (II Sam. 1), a lament which we should not doubt to be a sincere one. Nevertheless, David's grief does nothing to turn the followers of Saul away from him, just as is the case when David mourns the murder of Abner, Saul's commander. "All the peoples took notice of it," we are told in II Sam. 3:36, "and it pleased them; as everything that the king did pleased all the people."

David is, indeed, a master at consolidating his power. His estranged wife Michal is forced to return to his house, leaving behind her weeping but powerless second husband (II Sam. 3:12-16). David thus once more exhibits a legitimate connection with the house of Saul! This appearance is strengthened when David takes revenge on the murderers of Saul's son (II Sam. 4). Within seven and one half years, through the use of such shrewd measures, David, who had first been the king only of the southern tribe of Judah (II Sam. 2:4), wins over the followers of the northern house of Saul and becomes the undisputed ruler of all the tribes of Israel (II Sam. 5:3).

David is not through, however. He now sets about to establish a real kingdom. Perhaps his master stroke is to make Jerusalem his capital (II Sam. 5:6-10). This city had belonged neither to the northern nor southern tribes in Israel, but had been a Canaanite, Jebusite fortress. It therefore formed a middle, binding point between the traditionally divided north and south, and it lay on the main road which ran through Palestine. Best of all, the city was an almost impregnable fortress, surrounded by deep valleys on the west, east and south, and by hills to the north.

Having taken the city, David then ordered that the ark of the Lord be brought to it (II Sam. 6), again a measure which is not without political implications. Now religious authority is centered in the same place as the political and military authority, and David's claim to the throne is absolutized by giving it religious sanction.

At the same time, David establishes Israel's place as a nation among other nations in the ancient world by setting up commercial relations with Hiram of Tyre (II Sam. 5:11). It was a necessary step to maintain power in the ancient world, for Palestine had no harbors by which to carry on international trade. Tyre's seaports were necessary to support the Davidic monarchy, a monarchy capable of subduing not only the Philistines (II Sam. 5:25), but most of the surrounding peoples as well (II Sam. 8-9).

Then, like every other oriental monarch, David establishes a court, complete with harem (II Sam. 5:13), commander, chancellor, and foreign bodyguard. The royal scribe is one Seraiah or Shavsha, a Babylonian capable of writing the international language of Babylonian Accadian. And finally, to make the picture complete, David's own sons are established as priests for the people (II Sam. 8:15-18; I Chron. 18:14-17). Israel has come a long way from its primitive amphictyonic organization. David rules over all from "the city of David," and all power—political, military, and religious—is concentrated in his hands. It is little wonder that ever after Israel was to remember David's as the ideal reign.

At the height of his power, however, disaster strikes this King of Israel, and the story of his downfall comes to us from the pen of an eyewitness in his court. This eyewitness acount, which is found interspersed throughout II Sam. 6–I Kings 2, is unparalleled in the literature of the ancient Near East. For the first time in history, someone dares tell the truth about a king, not sensationally, not cheaply, but with dignity and restraint. In this story we learn not only about David the king. We learn also about David the man.

Again this story seems very secular in nature, and it tells quite simply how David sealed his own doom:

In the spring of the year, the time when kings go forth to battle, David sent Joab, and his servants with him, and all Israel; and they ravaged the Ammonites, and besieged Rabbah. But David remained at Jerusalem.

It happened, late one afternoon, when David arose from his couch and was walking upon the roof of the king's house, that he saw from the roof a woman bathing; and the woman was very beautiful. And David sent and inquired about the woman. And one said, "Is not this Bathsheba, the daughter of Eliam, the wife of Uriah the Hittite?" So David sent messengers, and took her; and she came to him, and he lay with her. . . . Then she returned to her house. And the woman conceived; and she sent and told David, "I am with child." (II Sam. 11:1-5.)

To hide the fact that he has committed adultery, David is forced to order the murder of Uriah, Bathsheba's husband. From this point on there starts a chain of evil which never ends for this King of Israel. "Thou shalt not kill. Thou shalt not

commit adultery. Thou shalt not steal. Thou shalt not covet."
(K.J.V.) Because of his desire for Bathsheba, the Messiah of
Yahweh breaks all of these commandments and thereby re-
leases upon himself the effects of his wrongdoing.

The results of David's sin with Bathsheba become evident
in his relations with his sons, for how can a father discipline
his children when he knows that he has done worse than
they? When David's son Amnon rapes Tamar (II Sam. 13),
we are told that David is very angry (II Sam. 13:21), and yet
David takes no action, for he, too, has committed his own
sexual offense. The upshot is that Tamar's brother, Absalom,
murders Amnon (II Sam. 13:29), but David again does nothing, for he, too, has a murder on his head. When Absalom
flees, David merely longs for that son's return (II Sam. 13:39),
and David finally welcomes the murderer back into his house
with a kiss (II Sam. 14:33). Then Absalom revolts and would
usurp the kingdom, but David is concerned only that his
son's life be spared. Indeed, so weak is David in ruling over
his sons and therefore also his realm, that when Absalom is
slain, David's commander Joab must rebuke him for his
attitude:

Then Joab came into the house to the king, and said, "You have
today covered with shame the faces of all your servants, who have
this day saved your life, and the lives of your sons and your daughters, and the lives of your wives and your concubines, because you
love those who hate you and hate those who love you. For you
have made it clear today that commanders and servants are nothing to you; for today I perceive that if Absalom were alive and
all of us were dead today, then you would be pleased." (II Sam.
19:5-6.)

94

Joab does not know that David cannot rule in his own house because he is burdened with his own guilt. Everything in the story of David's downfall can be explained on this basis, and seemingly God has had nothing to do with the disaster that has befallen Israel's king. David is a broken and penitent father, tearfully ascending the Mount of Olives (II Sam. 15: 30), and at the end of his life, he is a feeble and ineffective old man, who must be pampered and cuddled (I Kings 1:1-4). How thoroughly human and apart from God seems this Israelite Messiah! He is apparently a self-made man, who has also brought his own downfall.

4. GOD'S PROMISE TO DAVID AND ITS EFFECTS WITHIN HISTORY

(Read II Samuel 7; 23:1-7; Psalm 132)

The truth of the matter is that the story of David is not at all a secular one. Despite all of the rape and murder and revolt surrounding David's life, God still uses him for his purposes. We moderns are accustomed to finding God in peace and beauty and silence. The Old Testament most often knows him present behind the violence and flow and clatter of everyday life. For the God of the Bible is interested first of all in human history, in bringing that history to completion according to his will. Thus, the Old Testament witnesses to God's work in this history of David. God has guided its course, and the instrument of guidance has been, once again, his promise spoken to man.

In II Sam. 7, we find a promise given to David, a new addition to God's promise to Israel. The content of this promise is threefold, reflecting three different layers in the traditions collected together here. First of all, David is not to build

Yahweh a house, i.e. the temple, but Yahweh will build David a house (vss. 1-7, 11c). This is simply another way of saying that God here promises to establish the Davidic monarchy and to make it secure. No longer is the kingship under the judgment which tormented Saul. Now it is affirmed and made sure by God himself. Yahweh here approves the monarchical structure of Israel's life. This of course does not mean that the Lord has abdicated his kingship over Israel, for his sovereignty is forever certain. But rather now, just because Yahweh is king, he can guarantee David's throne. With all of the might of his universal sway, Yahweh promises to uphold Israel's king. In an older tradition in II Sam. 23:1-7, this is expressed by saying that Yahweh has made an everlasting covenant with David.

Secondly, however, in II Sam. 7:12-14, this promise given to David is extended to include David's heirs, and the implication is that an occupant for the Davidic throne will never be lacking (cf. Ps. 132:11-12). Yahweh will be a father to David's descendants, and they will be his sons. The germ of all messianic hopes in the Bible is contained in this promise, and it is in the light of it that Matthew was eager to proclaim that Jesus Christ was the Son of David (Matt. 1:1). God here binds himself never to cut off the Davidic line.

In the third place, the promise is extended to Israel, in II Sam. 7:24, and God's guarantee of the Davidic throne becomes also a guarantee of the life of David's people. Because Yahweh has entered into an everlasting relationship with David, he will also forever be Israel's God and they shall be his people. The existence of the Israelite nation is here given eternal validity.

To the original promise given to the patriarchs there is

added, then, this new promise. Just as the first promise meant that God began an action within history, so here, too, this word to David means that God begins another action. Having made them a great nation and entered into covenant with them and given them a land, Yahweh is by no means through with Israel. He presses on here by means of a new effective word toward his goal for mankind's history, his goal of restoring to rebellious mankind the goodness and blessing given at creation. As we shall see, this promise to David will also be a means to that end. Through a descendant of David and a son of Abraham God will bless all nations. Now both the patriarchal and monarchical traditions are included in the promise. God moves forward in his wondrous ways to fulfill his word.

We are given an indication of God's action only very rarely in David's own story. Indeed, like the promise to Abraham, this promise to David seems somewhat preposterous, for we have already been told in II Sam. 6:23 that David's wife, Michal, is barren. How can David's house endure forever if his wife bears him no sons? Somehow God uses the most unpleasant events to keep his promise to David, for it is the adulterous Bathsheba who must bear children for the king. We are told, moreover, that the child Solomon who is born of this unholy union is nevertheless the descendant of David who is loved by the Lord (II Sam. 12:24). God, it is clear, cannot be defeated by the evil in David's life. He uses it, molds it, despite man's sin, to accord with his purpose. Yahweh has sworn to David that he will give him successors to his throne. And the one that Yahweh loves and chooses is David's son Solomon!

But David has other sons who have first claim to the

throne, Amnon his first-born, and Absalom, and Adonijah. If God loves Solomon first of all, what is to become of these others? We know full well that Amnon and Absalom fall victim to their own evil and to their father's inability to curb them. Amnon is destroyed on the jagged rocks of his own passions. Absalom is overly ambitious for the throne and loses his life in his revolt. Then, at the last moment, when it seems that Adonijah will be made king (I Kings 1), Bathsheba and a prophet of God called Nathan intervene on behalf of Solomon. This one who is beloved by the Lord is placed on the Davidic throne (I Kings 1:39), and following David's death (I Kings 2:10), his reign is quickly secured. Adonijah, who still seeks power for himself by asking for David's concubine (I Kings 2:17 ff.), is quickly assassinated at the order of Solomon (I Kings 2:25). Abiathar, the priest who supported Adonijah, is banished from Jerusalem (I Kings 2:26-27). Joab, who also supported Adonijah, is killed in the tabernacle (I Kings 2:34). At the end of our eye-witness account, we have the final notice: "So the kingdom was established in the hand of Solomon" (I Kings 2:46).

The implication throughout this story is that no event, whether it be adultery or rape or murder or revolt has lain outside the purpose of Yahweh. God has not created these evils. They have been the result of man's own sin. But nevertheless, God has used them to accomplish his will. In the innermost workings of the human heart, in David's guilt and Amnon's lust and Absalom's ambition, God has seen his opportunity, and through the decisions and impulses of men, completely hidden from human eyes, he has worked his purpose. At the beginning of the story, he promises an heir to David. Then he sets his love upon Solomon as the one to be that heir, and all events work together to set Solomon upon the throne. Far from being secular in nature, this Old Testament story witnesses to the fact that there is no realm in human life, no matter how dark and ugly it may be, in which God is not actively present and working to move history forward toward his goal. It is little wonder that such a God found in a criminal's cross, smeared with blood and sweat, his supreme opportunity to work his purpose in the world. This God had been dealing with man's darkest moments for centuries before Calvary.

5. THE PROMISE TO DAVID AND THE MESSIANIC HOPES OF ISRAEL

(Read Psalms 2, 18, 20, 21, 45, 72, 89, 101, 110, 132)

God's promise to David had an extraordinary effect upon Israel's view of himself. Now the people's life was totally bound up with that of its king. It was to the Davidic ruler that God had made a promise to preserve his line forever, and this meant that the king's people also shared in this eternal guarantee. As long as a descendant of David sat upon the throne, Israel could be sure that God's favor was upon them. As long as all was well with the king, all would be well with Israel.

In other words, the king of Israel now became the embodiment of the people's life as a whole. If the king exercised justice and faithfulness and righteousness in his rule over his people, as we read in Ps. 18 or 101 or 45:6-7, then his people, too, were considered good in God's eyes and would be blessed by the Lord. But if the king sinned, then the whole nation fell under the judgment of God, as is the case in the story of David in II Sam. 24. God's rejection of the king was at the same time a rejection of Israel as a whole (Ps. 89).

Israel's hopes for its future, therefore, came to be centered in large measure around the person of its anointed king, of its "Messiah," which is simply a transliteration of the Hebrew word for "anointed." The people felt that if they had a perfect king, then all the blessings of God would be bestowed upon them in full measure. As we can see clearly in Ps. 72, these blessings would include not only the intangible gifts of peace and security within the community of Israel, but also material gifts—abundance of crops, and prosperous citizens, and fertile fields and homes. Furthermore, Israel's place among the world of nations would be made secure. The reign of the ideal sovereign would bring what the Old Testament calls *shalom* to Israel, i.e., all good, all peace, all blessing, all prosperity, life in its fullness. Israel, in short, looked forward to a return of the original goodness of creation, and the instrument for bringing this condition of blessedness to Israel would be God's anointed king. When the perfect Messiah ascended the throne, he would, in Isaiah's words, be "the shadow of a mighty rock within a weary land" (Isa. 32:2 E. C. Clephane translation). Jeremiah concurred: "In his days Judah will be saved, and Israel will dwell securely" (Jer. 23:6).

To each king who ascended the throne, Israel hopefully ascribed perfection. Above all, the king's intimate relationship with Yahweh was stressed. The king was Yahweh's adopted son (Ps. 2:7; cf. 89:26), enjoying a unique relationship with him. He sat at the right hand of Yahweh (Ps. 110:1) and was in constant communion with him (Ps. 2:8; 20:1-4; 21:1-7). Sometimes he sat on the throne of Yahweh himself and acted as Yahweh's mandator (Ps. 110:5). All this was meant to express the fact that the king was in perfect communion with

100

God and that therefore he could be a channel of God's blessing to his people Israel.

Because the king enjoyed such an intimate relationship with the Lord, he also shared God's power, and God gave to him universal rule over all nations. He was girded and strengthened for war by Yahweh himself, and through the help of Yahweh, he was able to conquer all of his enemies (Ps. 18; 20; 21; 45; 110; cf. Num. 23:24; 24:8, 17-19). But again this meant that Israel would share in such victory. Indeed, there would be no evil which could be brought upon Israel (Num. 23:8, 20-23), and the military triumph and perfection of his king would bring in for him an era of golden peace and blessedness (Num. 23:9-10; 24:5-7).

To be sure, none of these ascriptions of perfection, which we have in the Psalms and which were probably composed by court prophets, ever fitted the actual historical occupants of Israel's throne. As we see from the phrasing in Ps. 72, such ascriptions were wishes, stereotypes, hopes attached to the royal office. All were dependent on the king's actually reigning among his people in justice and righteousness and acceptability before God. Only as the king stood perfectly in relationship with the Lord would these glowing hopes attached to him become reality.

With each new king, Israel hoped anew. He hoped that this one would be God's perfect Messiah, the one who would bring in the golden age. Of each of its kings, Israel asked, "Are you the one who is to come, or shall we look for another?" From the time of David onward, Israel expected a ruler who would save his people, a ruler who would restore to them all of the goodness of the creation.

It is for this reason that one of the two great historical

works which we have in the Old Testament, the deuteronomic history, which runs from Genesis through II Kings and which was edited by a single school of authors in the sixth century B.C., ends with a notice about the release of King Jehoiachin from his prison in Babylonian exile (II Kings 25:27-30). The authors of this history are telling a defeated and exiled Israel that a descendant of David still lives. God yet preserves alive the bearer of the promise to David, and thus there is still hope that the expected Messiah will come. As long as the seed of David is preserved, Israel has a hope for the future. The perfect king may yet bring in the day of Israel's blessedness, the day when the nation will be exalted and dwell in peace and security.

It is to the fulfillment of this messianic hope that the New Testament refers when it says that Jesus Christ was the Son of David (Matt. 1:1; Luke 1:27; 2:4; Rom. 1:3; 2 Tim. 2:8; Rev. 5:5; 22:16). And on the day that Jesus rode into Jerusalem, the crowd that welcomed him saw in him the long-awaited Davidic deliverer (Matt. 21:9), the one who would restore the kingdom to Israel (Acts 1:6). But our Lord represented a different kind of Messiah and a different kind of kingdom than those expected by the Jews. His was a kingship and a kingdom foretold by the prophets, and to their proclamation we now must turn to complete our story of Israel.

CHAPTER VI

The Prophetic Understanding of the Promise

1. THE FAITH OF ISRAEL UNDER THE MONARCHY
(Read I Kings 12–II Kings 25)

When we look back over Israel's history as a monarchy, it seems surprising that the Hebrew people ever felt secure during the turbulent centuries from the death of David in 961 B.C. to the final fall of Judah in 587 B.C. Solomon's reign, for all of its glory, laid heavy burdens on the people's life, draining their economy and strength through taxation and forced labor for the sake of the royal building projects and elaborate court. When Solomon died in 922, traditional jealousies between north and south split his kingdom in two, and Israel and Judah thereafter often weakened themselves by warring against one another.

Then, too, external enemies constantly harassed the Hebrew monarchies. The ninth century brought with it almost constant warfare with Aram, warfare which abated only when Assyria attacked Aram on another front. Moreover, Israel and Judah, too, at times fell victim to the growing

Assyrian giant. It was only briefly during the first half of the eight century B.C. that either kingdom found political and military respite from its troubles, during the reigns of Jeroboam II in Israel and of Uzziah in Judah.

It is significant, however, that the first of the classical prophets, Amos, was active during the reign of Jeroboam II, for although Israel and Judah had peace without, there was little harmony within. Relatively stable international conditions allowed the influx of wealth into the Hebrew kingdoms, and this brought with it a class stratification of Hebrew society. The rich grew richer, the poor grew poorer, and injustice was rife, the wealthy and powerful exploiting the peasants for their own ends. After the death of Jeroboam, revolutions and plots swirled round the throne of the northern kingdom, and these were ended only by the resurgence of Assyrian power.

In 745 B.C., Tiglath-pileser III took over the rule of Assyria, and from that time on, Israel and Judah were never again free from the threat of empires from Mesopotamia. In 721 B.C., the northern kingdom of Israel fell to the Assyrian conqueror Sargon II. Its peoples were exiled to the region of "Gozan, and in the cities of the Medes" (II Kings 17:6), and the populace was replaced with settlers from Babylonia, Elam, and Aram. In 701, Judah tried to throw off the Assyrian yoke, with the consequence that Sennacherib of Assyria devastated and reduced the country. It was not until the last quarter of the seventh century B.C., when Assyrian power declined, that Judah was able again to assert itself, under the wise King Josiah.

Living as it did, however, in the international corridor of the world, Judah could not escape the armies and conflicts of empire. The year 626 marked the emergence of Babylonian power, and Judah was caught in the rivalry of Babylonia with Egypt. Josiah lost his life in 609 B.C., in a battle against the Pharaoh Necho, and Judah was briefly subject to Egyptian rule, only to have those rulers replaced by the Babylonians. But Egyptian intrigue kept the spirit of revolt alive in the southern kingdom, and the final result was the complete overthrow of Judah and Jerusalem by the Babylonian Nebuchadnezzar in 587 B.C.

It can truly be said that during almost four hundred years of monarchy, the Hebrew people never once really had cause for complacency. Their life was constantly threatened by war or revolution or class injustice and unrest. At no time during the history of either Israel or Judah could we ever say all was well. At no time did they ever enjoy true stability and peace.

And yet, fantastic as it may seem, this was a people who were sure that God was with them! Much as the modern Christian wrestles with the problems of cold war and hot war, of prejudice and social injustice, of defense and peace, in the security that nevertheless God is on his side, so the Hebrew people struggled with their problems in history in the assurance that God had not deserted them.

They were quick to acknowledge from time to time, as for example in the religious reforms of Hezekiah (II Kings 18: 4-6) or Josiah (II Kings 22-23), that there were religious and social wrongs which needed to be corrected. Indeed, there was no period in Israel's life as a monarchy when a prophetic or a reforming voice was not heard, urging the redress of evils which had corrupted the communal and political life. And yet, the Hebrew community was confident that it abided in Yahweh's favor and that confession of its shortcomings would easily lead it into forgiveness:

105

Come, let us return to the Lord;
  for he has torn, that he may heal us;
  he has stricken, and he will bind us up.
After two days he will revive us;
  on the third day he will raise us up,
  that we may live before him.
Let us know, let us press on to know the Lord;
  his going forth is sure as the dawn;
he will come to us as the showers,
  as the spring rains that water the earth.

(Hos. 6:1-3.)

The basis for this confidence Israel found, as does the modern-day church, in its past history with Yahweh. It was the very mercy and grace of God which Israel had experienced in the past which made him certain that God would never desert him in the future. After all, Israel was the people of the promise! Yahweh had sworn to Abraham that Israel would be the means whereby he would bless all nations. This meant that Israel's history had been given an absolute goal. God would not, indeed, could not, destroy his people or let them be annihilated, for God then would have no instrument by which to fulfill his word.

We find contained within the prophetic writings expressions of this confidence on the part of the Israelite populace. The people tell Amos that the Lord, the God of hosts, will be with them (cf. Amos 5:14). Their conclusion is therefore, "Evil shall not overtake or meet us" (Amos 9:10). When Micah preaches to them of doom, they reply, "One should not preach of such things; disgrace will not overtake us" (Mic. 2:6). Indeed, much as the modern Christian feels himself to be working out his own destiny in the world, so the Israelites under the monarchy felt that Yahweh was an innocent by-stander to their activities. "The Lord will not do good, nor will he do ill," they thought (Zeph. 1:12). Gone was the belief that God was working in their times, or at least the faith that he was doing anything other than supporting and comforting his own. "He will do nothing," the people reassured themselves, "no evil will come upon us, nor shall we see sword or famine" (Jer. 5:12).

That such religious complacency was fostered by Yahweh's gifts of the law and the kingship and the cultic revelation of himself can also not be doubted. "We are wise, and the law of the Lord is with us," was the smug boast of the people who heard Jeremiah (Jer. 8:8). The fact that Yahweh had graciously given his people his commandments was regarded as a sign of his everlasting favor. Again, the presence of the temple in which Yahweh revealed himself and was believed to dwell was thought to be the magical guarantee of the inviolability of Zion (cf. Jer. 7:4). "Who shall come down against us, or who shall enter our habitations?" (Jer. 21:13.) "Thou, O Lord, art in the midst of us, and we are called by thy name." (Jer. 14:9.) "Is not the Lord in the midst of us? No evil shall come upon us." (Mic. 3:11.) When some disaster overtook the holy city of Jerusalem, it was an incomprehensible event, for there dwelt both Yahweh and the Davidic king, within the royal temple and palace enclosure, and the presence of God and of his chosen royal son were supposedly guarantees against all misfortune (Jer. 8:19; Mic. 4:9).

In short, it was the faith of Israel in the time of the monarchies that Yahweh's promises and past actions of mercy were eternal warranties for the future. God had given promises to Abraham and David which Israel thought insured their security forever. Yahweh could not abandon Israel because he had bound himself to his people with his word. The people of the old covenant, often like those of the modern new covenant, believed that they were indispensable to God. Yahweh, they trusted, would be with them "even unto the end of the world" (K.J.V.).

2. THE PROPHETIC REAFFIRMATION OF THE LORDSHIP OF YAHWEH

(*Read Amos, Hosea, Isaiah 1-12, 28-31, Jeremiah 1-29*)

It was the prophetic voice in Israel which proclaimed what it meant to be "with Yahweh," and to a people grown complacent about the divine presence, it was the prophets, throughout the years of the monarchy, who made his lordship once again vividly real. For the basis of much of their preaching, the prophets drew on no new concepts. Rather they reaffirmed the nature of the service to which Israel had pledged himself when he entered into covenant with his God. One thing, however, distinguished the prophets from those to whom they preached: they spoke out of a burning personal awareness of the nature of the God of history. God's hand was upon them, his word was in their mouths, his commandment burned like a fire within their bones. The prophets were, in truth, men overcome by an unseen Companion, and this One who was with them they knew also to be Israel's Lord. To be "with Yahweh" meant to be subject to his lordship. From the earliest to the latest times, this covenant fact formed much of the content of the prophetic proclamation.

For example, the prophets preached that Israel could not worship the gods of the Canaanites or of the Phoenicians or of the Mesopotamians and still claim to be Yahweh's. "How long will you go limping with two different opinions?" challenged Elijah on Mount Carmel. "If the Lord is God, follow him; but if Baal, then follow him." (I Kings 18:21.) The God whom Israel had sworn to serve in covenant faithfulness was either absolute Lord or nothing to Israel. His people could not serve him and every idol of the ancient world as well. To have God with them meant that Israel had to give him absolute loyalty.

This loyalty, moreover, was not to be limited to the practice of worship and devotions. It involved Israel's daily bread and his manner of politics. As Hosea repeatedly proclaimed, Israel could not worship the great god Nature as the source of his food supply and yet profess that he thanked and counted on Yahweh for every gift in life. Nor could he run to Egypt or Assyria for military alliances and still maintain that Yahweh's protection was his all in all. Amos, Hosea, Isaiah, and Jeremiah made it clear that God was to be Lord in these areas of life, too, and indeed, that there was no part of Israel's life over which Yahweh was not to be sole ruler.

The land upon which Israel lived had been the gift of God. Its cultivation and care, therefore, were subject to God's commands, as can be seen quite clearly in the laws of Lev. 25. But more, God would take back his land if his absolute lordship were not acknowledged. This is seen most clearly in a passage from Ezekiel:

The word of the Lord came to me: "Son of man, the inhabitants of these waste places in the land of Israel keep saying, 'Abraham was only one man, yet he got possession of the land; but we are many; the land is surely given us to possess.' Therefore say to them, Thus says the Lord God: You eat flesh with the blood, and lift up your eyes to your idols, and shed blood; shall you then possess the land? You resort to the sword, you commit abominations and each of you defiles his neighbor's wife; shall you then possess the land? Say this to them, Thus says the Lord God: As I live . . . I will make the land a desolation and a waste; and her proud might shall come to an end; and the mountains of Israel shall be so desolate that none will pass through. Then they will know that I am the Lord, when I have made the land a desolation and a waste because of all their abominations which they have committed."

(Ezek. 33:23-29.)

There was, in fact, no gift which Yahweh had given to his people which was not subject to the regulation of Israel's Lord, and among these gifts was included that of the kingship itself. No Ahab, with a cunning Jezebel at his side, could successfully defy the divine King over Judah, not even when that defiance concerned merely Naboth's little vineyard which adjoined the royal grounds (I Kings 21). For the sake of Naboth, God and his prophets toppled the royal dynasty (I Kings 21:20 ff.; II Kings 9). And as we see so clearly in the prophetic pronouncements to the Davidic kings in Jer. 21 and 22, these royal sons of Yahweh, too, were expected to be subservient to Yahweh's demands for justice and righteousness.

In short, it was the prophets in Israel who placed once again before the chosen people the demands of the covenant relation. To be God's people Israel had agreed to be subject to his transcendant will. Moreover, they had said that they would live as members of a community regulated solely by the will of God. It is not surprising therefore that the prophets preached about ethics. They were simply giving voice to the commandments of God for his community. The oppression of the poor against which Amos spoke (2:6-7; 4:1; 5:10 ff.) or the corruption and injustice pictured by Isaiah (1:21-23; 3: 13-15; 5; et al.) were far from the harmony and brotherhood required by God of his people. The prophets introduced no new ethical teachings into the Israelite scene. Rather they called for true compliance to the will of Israel's covenant Lord. And like the Mosaic traditions before them, they often found this will in the law.

It has been a modern error in dealing with the Old Testament to contrast the ethical religion of the prophets with the supposed legalism of Israel's earlier periods. Many have thought to find in the prophetic writings a new and higher step in the development of Israelite faith and thought. But the truth is that the prophets, too, saw in the law an expression of God's will for his people. They constantly chastized the people for their disobedience of the law. In Amos 2:4, the judgment of the Lord is directed against Judah, because "they have rejected the law of the Lord, and have not kept his statutes." In Hos. 4:6, it is proclaimed that the people are destroyed for lack of knowledge of their God, and the blame for this is laid upon the priest who was supposed to teach the law and yet who has forgotten it (cf. Jer. 2:8; Zeph. 3:4; Ezek. 7:26). Isa. 1:10 proclaims, "Give ear to the torah [law] of our God, you people of Gomorrah (Hebrew)!" When it is asked, "Why is the land ruined and laid waste like a wilderness, so that no one passes through?" (Jer. 9:12) the Lord replies, "Because they have forsaken my law which I set before them, and have not obeyed my voice, or walked in accord with it" (Jer. 9:13). These examples of the prophetic affirmation of the law could be multiplied many times over.

It is most important to realize, however, that it was the

prophets who attempted to make real once again for Israel the basic relationship of the covenant, the relationship in which Yahweh was sovereign Lord and Israel was his servant. The prophets were preachers against idolatry, against disobedience to the law, against social injustice and immorality because all of these were contradictions of Yahweh's will for his covenant community, and it was to that sovereign will alone that the covenant community was responsible. The prophets were not ethical monotheists or social reformers or pacifistic politicians or puritanical legalists. They were heralds of the sole lordship of Yahweh. In every area of Israel's life that lordship was to be made manifest. If Yahweh was with Israel, then he was with them as their Ruler. The God of the Bible accepts no other status in his relationship with his people!

It was in this context that the prophets also attacked the worship and cultic practices of their day. Just as it is false to believe that the prophets substituted an ethical religion for a legalistic one, so it is equally erroneous to believe that they were the pioneers of a purely spiritual worship over against the Israelite cult and sacrifice. Had the contemporary temple cult and offering been true signs of devotion to the Lord, the prophets would have had no quarrel with Israel's worship life (cf. Hagg., Mal. 1-2). But the truth of the matter is that Israel's worship had become a mockery of God's rule.

The Hebrew people loved to go to church. We hear in Amos of sacrifices every morning, of tithes every three days, of thanksgivings of leavened bread and the publication of freewill offerings. (Amos 4:4-5). Moreover, worship was a joyful affair. There were songs and harps in the sanctuary (Amos 5:23), days of feasts and Sabbath celebrations (Hos. 2:11), times when the people packed the temple, and prayers so numerous as to weary Yahweh's soul (Isa. 1:12-15).

But all was carried on with no conception of the will and person of the God being worshiped. In his famous temple sermon in chapter seven, Jeremiah tells us that the people stole, murdered, committed adultery, swore falsely, burned incense to the nature god Baal, went after other gods, and then came and stood before Yahweh in the temple and declared, "We are delivered"! There was no realization on the people's part that Yahweh laid demands upon them, no recognition that he was a Lord they were to serve, no awareness of the fact that religion is more than comfort and that the "worship experience" is never an end in itself. Israel had lost all sense of its relationship to its personal Lord, and for this reason its very worship was a sin (Amos 4:4-5) which Yahweh hated to the core of his soul:

> I hate, I despise your feasts,
>   and I take no delight in your solemn assemblies.
> Even though you offer me your burnt offerings and
>   cereal offerings,
>   I will not accept them,
> and the peace offerings of your fatted beasts
>   I will not look upon.
> Take away from me the noise of your songs;
>   to the melody of your harps I will not listen.
> But let justice roll down like waters,
>   and righteousness like an everflowing stream.
>   (Amos 5:21-24; cf. Isa. 1:10-17.)

That which Yahweh required of his worshipers, the prophets preached, was surrender to his rule, a surrender made manifest in every area of life. As Hosea 6:6 puts it, "I desire steadfast love and not sacrifice, the knowledge of God, rather than burnt offerings." That is to say, God asks of his people when they pray that they know he is the Lord and that they let him rule constantly over their lives. He is not satisfied with thousands of rams for burnt offerings, Micah tells us, or ten thousand rivers of oil. Even a first-born son would be insufficient as an atoning sacrifice. Rather that which Yahweh requires is justice to one's fellow men within God's community, covenant love and faithfulness to one's divine ruler, and constant surrender in walking every moment with one's God (Mic. 6:6-8).

Worship in the prophets is never a good in itself. It is not required by Yahweh for its own sake nor is it automatically efficacious. It is not required in order that Israel may enter into a mystical experience of his God. Israel is not asked to worship in order to gain strength for his daily life. Indeed, worship in the prophets is not even the source of knowledge of God, for Israel is to know his God from God's actions in history. Rather, worship is for the prophets a visible sign of an inner surrender, the outward manifestation of total capitulation to Yahweh's rule. Those who love the Lord will worship at his altar, but without the dedication of oneself to God, worship is a mockery. As it is put in Ps. 40:6-7, God requires not sacrifice or offering, but the affirmation, "Lo, I come." Or as we read in Ps. 51:16-17:

> Thou hast no delight in sacrifice;
>   were I to give a burnt offering, thou wouldst not
>   be pleased.
> The sacrifice acceptable to God is a broken spirit;

a broken and contrite heart, O God, thou wilt not
despise.

It is only the complete surrender of the worshiper to Yahweh
which makes up true worship in the Bible. It is only those who
know him as Lord who may come before his throne of glory.

Over every realm of Israel's life the prophets saw Yahweh
to be ruler, and no action was to lie outside his sovereign
sway. Worship, politics, agriculture, business, and communal
ethics—all were to be subject to the will of God, for Yahweh
was covenant Lord of Israel and Israel was his servant.

It is the genius of the classical prophets, a genius born
of their own personal knowledge of God, that they appre-
hend what constitutes true surrender to the Lord. For all of
their mention of the law and of ethics, the prophets set before
Israel no codes of behavior and morality. They do not see
surrender to God to be exhausted by conformity to the Ten
Commandments, and the prophets posit no virtues after which
Israel is to strive. In other words, the prophets are not
preachers of religious ideals.

Rather, they know surrender to the Lord to be a matter of
inward, intimate relationship to a personal God. In a man's
heart and will and motivation the prophets find the source of
religion, and it is an inward surrender, manifested in outward
faithfulness, to the Lord which the prophets ask of their
people.

Throughout the prophetic writings, therefore, we find the
most intimate figures used to portray the relationship between
Israel and his God. In Hosea, Yahweh is Israel's husband,
Israel is his wife, and the relationship between them is to be
one of marital intimacy, marked by the faithfulness and love

of a couple who know and cling to each other from the depths of their souls. Yahweh has betrothed Israel by bringing her out of Egypt (Hos. 13:5). Israel is asked to live with her divine husband in faithfulness and knowledge and love (cf. Ezek. 16).

In Jeremiah, and also again in Hosea, Yahweh is pictured as the Father of Israel, and as in the Exodus traditions, Israel is his son (Hos. 11:1; cf. Isa. 1:2). This is a son whom Yahweh loves dearly, and over whose future he dreams:

> Is Ephraim my dear son?
> Is he my darling child?
> For as often as I speak against him,
> I do remember him still.
> > (Jer. 31:20.)

> I thought how I would set you among my sons,
> and give you a pleasant land,
> a heritage most beauteous of all nations.
> And I thought you would call me, My Father,
> and would not turn from following me.
> > (Jer. 3:19.)

Israel is asked to respond to Yahweh with the love and knowledge of a son for his father.

In Isaiah, the key word is faith, faith in an incomparable Ruler, and Judah is asked to place his international life and fortune in the hands of the Holy God. When King Ahaz of Judah is threatened by the armies of Israel and Syria, Isaiah tells him that faith alone will save him: "If you will not believe, surely you shall not be established" (Isa. 7:9). When Hezekiah looks to alliance with Egypt to free himself from the Assyrian yoke, Isaiah proclaims, "In returning and rest you shall be saved; in quietness and in trust shall be your strength" (Isa. 30:15). Isaiah's call to his people is to abandon reliance on other helpers (Isa. 31:1, 3) and to grasp hold of the unseen hand of God in trust and surrender to his rule. "Take heed, be quiet, do not fear, and do not let your heart be faint." (Isa. 7:4.) Such is Isaiah's foreign policy. It is a policy founded on complete knowledge and trust of the goodness and power of God.

These prophets ask of their people, as did Deuteronomy who drew on their teachings, essentially that they surrender to God because they know and love him. Continually the prophets recall God's acts of mercy in the past. They bring to remembrance the Exodus and God's guidance in the wilderness (Amos 2:9-10; Hos. 13:4-5; Jer. 2:2-3). They recall that Yahweh has given his people a land flowing with milk and honey (Jer. 2:7; 32:22; Ezek. 20:6). They remind their hearers that God has chosen them out of all of the people on the earth (Amos 3:2; Ezek. 16:8). They affirm the fact that the Davidic house and the city of David are precious to the Lord (Isa. 38:5; 37:35; 31:4-9, et al., cf. Jer. 22:6, 24). The call of the prophets is therefore the call to respond to this love in kind, to surrender in gratitude and trust, in faithfulness and knowledge to the God who has blessed them their life long. "Circumcise yourselves to the Lord," Jeremiah tells Judah, "remove the foreskin of your hearts" (Jer. 4:4). "Get yourselves a new heart and a new spirit," Ezekiel begs his people (Ezek. 18:31). The prophets know that surrender to God is a matter of the inward man. They ask of the covenant people that they love the Lord with their whole heart and soul and mind. When this demand is met, ethics and morality will follow after, and each Israelite will also love his neighbor as himself.

Jesus affirms this total tradition when he tells us that on the two great commandments, the command to love God and to love neighbor, depend all the law and the prophets (Matt. 22:36-40). Truly, that which both law and prophets teach is the inner surrender of love, the surrender of our whole selves to God's lordship over every realm of our lives. It was this surrender which the prophets of Israel required in the name of Yahweh. It is this surrender which God ever requires of his church.

3. THE SIN OF ISRAEL: HIS REBELLION AGAINST HIS COVENANT LORD

(Read Ezekiel 1-24; Micah 1-3; 6; Zephaniah)

It is the tragedy of the people of the old covenant that they were tried by the God of the prophets and found wanting. The Israelite community was supremely confident in the time of the monarchy that it lived in God's favor. The judgment of the prophets was that it was totally odious to God.

Throughout every realm of Israelite life, Yahweh failed to find any evidence that his people acknowledged his lordship. Israel's love for her divine husband was "like a morning cloud, like the dew that goes early away" (Hos. 6:4). She knew no faithfulness or covenant love for Yahweh (Hos. 4:1). She was as separated from God as an adulterous wife is from her husband (Hos. 5:4). Israel was, in another figure, a stupid child without understanding (Jer. 4:22), a son completely rebellious against his father's will (Hos. 11:2; Isa. 1:2). Gone from Yahweh's people was all inward devotion to him. They were a community which honored him with their lips, while their hearts were far from him (Isa. 29:13). They were a people who deliberately rejected their relationship with God.

It is the prophetic view of sin that it consists in a willful refusal to allow God to be the Lord of life, and thus, sin in its basic essentials is rebellion against Yahweh. It is a deliberate turning away from the relationship of love and faith and gratitude, a deliberate defiance of the Lord of mercy. So in Jeremiah, Judah has a stubborn and rebellious heart (Jer. 5:23; 18:12). The people are like bronze and iron (Jer. 6:28), refusing to return to Yahweh (Jer. 8:5 ff.), refusing to know him (Jer. 9:6), refusing to hear his words (Jer. 13:10). "They have made their faces harder than rock; they have refused to repent." (Jer. 5:3.) In Zephaniah,

> [Jerusalem] is rebellious and defiled,
>   the oppressing city!
> She listens to no voice,
>   she accepts no correction.
> She does not trust in the Lord,
>   she does not draw near to her God.
>   (Zeph. 3:1-2.)

In Ezekiel, the people have eyes to see, but see not, have ears to hear, but hear not. They are a completely corrupted and rebellious house (Ezek. 12:1-3). Indeed, it is the judgment of the prophets that Israel is laden with iniquity, a nation which has despised and forsaken its Lord and become utterly estranged from him (Isa. 1:4).

> The whole head is sick,
>   and the whole heart faint.
> From the sole of the foot even to the head,

119

there is no soundness in it,
but bruises and sores
   and bleeding wounds;
they are not pressed out, or bound up,
   or softened with oil.

(Isa. 1:5-6.)

The fact that the prophets understand sin to consist in a willful turning away from the personal relationship to Yahweh does not, however, lessen their apprehension of the fact that sin is a mysterious and demonic force which holds men in its grasp. Rebellion against God is man's own personal responsibility, as we see so clearly in Ezek. 18, and yet such rebellion is an unnatural thing, defying all of the laws of nature and of life:

Can a maiden forget her ornaments,
   or a bride her attire?
Yet my people have forgotten me
   days without number.

(Jer. 2:32.)

Does the snow of Lebanon leave
   the crags of Sirion?
Do the mountain waters run dry,
   the cold flowing streams?
But my people have forgotten me.

(Jer. 18:14-15.)

Even the stork in the heavens
   knows her times;
and the turtledove, swallow, and crane
   keep the time of their coming;

120

> but my people know not
> the ordinance of the Lord.
>
> (Jer. 8:7.)

Sin so warps a man's understanding that he becomes completely unaware of his faults. He maintains that he is not defiled (Jer. 2:23), that he is innocent and has not sinned (Jer. 2:35). Far from being ashamed of his actions, he does not even know how to blush (Jer. 6:15). He never asks what it is he has done, but plunges like a horse, headlong into battle (Jer. 8:6). And then when he gets into trouble, he thinks the Lord is still with him, and he cries out to God in desperation, "Arise and save us" (Jer. 2:27; cf. Hos. 6:1-3; 8:2).

Not only do the prophets understand that sin lames a man's power of self-criticism, but they also know that rebellion against God maims and weakens the will. It is the prophetic belief that throughout Israel's history, Yahweh has tried to correct and discipline his people in an effort to turn them aside from their evil course. In the Book of Amos, we read that God has used natural catastrophes in order to warn his people (Amos 4:6-10). Isaiah understands military defeats to have been instruments of Yahweh's discipline (Isa. 9:13; cf. Amos 4:11). And, of course, Yahweh has always sent his prophets to inform the people of his true will (Jer. 7:25-26). The prophets were set as watchmen over Israel, to warn of the consequences of sin, just as military sentinels warn of a coming enemy (Jer. 6:17; Ezek. 33:1-9; 3:16-21). But the people have persistently refused to listen to these prophets (Jer. 7:13, 27-28; 25:3-7; Zeph. 3:2). Sometimes they have killed them (Jer. 2:30), other times thrown them in prison (Jer. 38). Often they have been mocked or made the object of scorn

(Isa. 28). The will of Israel to do good has been so distorted by sin that the people are no longer capable of heeding Yahweh's word or of profiting from his guidance. "Their deeds do not permit them to return to their God," says Hosea (5:4), "for the spirit of harlotry is within them, and they know not the Lord."

In the prophetic view, Israel's sin is irremovable (Mic. 1:9), and though the people wash themselves with lye and use much soap, as Jeremiah puts it (Jer. 2:22), they cannot remove the stain of their guilt before God. It is hopeless to expect that they will return to Yahweh (Jer. 2:25), for they have lost all power for repentance and return. Their will and desire to return have been completely blunted. They are like a filthy and corroded copper pot, which cannot be cleaned, even with fire, and Yahweh merely wears himself out trying to purify them (Ezek. 24:9-13).

> Can the Ethiopian change his skin
>   or the leopard his spots?
> Then also you can do good
>   who are accustomed to do evil.
> (Jer. 13:23.)

This rebellion against Yahweh on Israel's part did not begin only in the time of the monarchy, however. It is the view of the prophets that Israel's whole history has been one of sin against her covenant Lord. Hosea and Jeremiah consider Israel's time in the desert to have been the time of her honeymoon with Yahweh (Hos. 2:15; Jer. 2:2), and her entrance into the land marked the beginning of her adultery. But Ezek. 20 and 23 assert that Israel's disobedience began even when she was in Egypt. Her entire history has been one of corruption and defiance of her Lord. Thus, the prophetic preaching now brings to light a rebellion against God which has been present in Israel from the first (cf. Hos. 12:2-3; Acts 7:2-53, especially vss. 51-53). All of Israel is related, past and present, by its common revolt against its Lord.

This is no longer a people holy and separated to Yahweh. This is no kingdom of priests, fit to mediate God's blessing to all of the peoples on the face of the earth. This is a rebel, like the rest of mankind, standing over against God. The son of God has denied his Father. He is a son no longer.

4. THE DESTRUCTION OF ISRAEL: YAHWEH'S EXERCISE OF HIS LORDSHIP IN JUDGMENT

To a people who were certain that they stood in the divine favor because Yahweh had given them a promise, to a nation which was sure that God was with them, the prophets now proclaimed an awful message. Yahweh would be with them, indeed, but he was coming to his people as a destroyer. Because they had rebelled against him, he would blot them from the face of the earth. Israel's sin was not a matter of some error or mistake standing in the way of the realization of Yahweh's lordship. It was complete rebellion against that lordship, complete rejection of Yahweh as Ruler of Israel's life, complete opposition to the God of history. That sin could only be corrected by totally wiping it out. "As I live, says the Lord God, surely with a mighty hand and an outstretched arm, and with wrath poured out, I will be king over you." (Ezek. 20:33.) Precisely because Yahweh is Lord of his people, they cannot revolt against him and live. He will manifest his sovereignty over them by destroying their rebellious life.

It is this prophetic proclamation of Yahweh's total judg-

ment on Israel which forms, along with the prophetic escha-
tology which we shall discuss in the next chapter, the unique
element in the preaching of the classical prophets. As we have
seen, they introduced no new ideas of God but rather reaffirmed the lordship of Yahweh which had been known to
Israel since the covenant on Sinai. In such reaffirmation they
differed little from the earlier prophets, such as Elijah and
Elisha, who had preceded them. But this part of their message was new, the message that God was breaking into Israel's
history with a new action, an action of the most radical kind.
Yahweh was coming to destroy his chosen people. Israel had
never heard that before.

The certainty that God was coming in awful judgment
was given to the classical prophets in their calls. Amos heard
the Lord roaring from Zion and saw the pastures and mountains wither before his voice (Amos 1:2). Isaiah received the
fearful commission to preach

> Until cities lie waste
>   without inhabitant,
> and houses without men,
>   and the land is utterly desolate,
> and the Lord removes men far away,
>   and the forsaken places are many in the midst
>   of the land.
>
> (Isa. 6:11-12.)

Jeremiah was given to see a boiling pot, with evil bubbling out
of it from the north (Jer. 1:13-14). To Micah was revealed
that the Lord was coming forth out of his place and that all
would melt before him like wax before the fire (Mic. 1:3-4).
Zephaniah saw God preparing a terrible sacrifice in which

124

the blood of men would be poured out like dust, and their flesh like dung (Zeph. 1). The prophets were commissioned by God to announce the beginning of his judgment, to release into history his destroying word of wrath.

The fearfulness of the judgment which the prophets announce is almost overwhelming in its immensity, and it is doubtful that we could find in any other literature so many figures of destruction as we find in the prophetic writings. Yahweh will summon against his people not only the fly of Egypt or the bee of Assyria (Isa. 7:18 ff.) or some mysterious destroyer from the north (Jer. 6:22 ff.), but he will also send against them the plagues of Sheol (Hos. 13:14) and deadly diseases (Jer. 16:4) and an overwhelming scourge (Isa. 28:18). He will turn nature against the people, so that the land will heave up and fall, like the rising and sinking of the Nile (Amos 8:8). The sun will go down at noon, and the earth will be darkened in broad daylight (Amos 8:9). Hail will strip the people (Isa. 28:17), waters will overflow them (cf. Isa. 8:5 ff.), and when the judgment is over, Zion will look like a plowed field (Mic. 3:12). Her birds and beasts will have fled and gone, and she will be nothing but a lair for jackals (Jer. 9:10-11). Indeed, in the thought of Jeremiah, Yahweh's judgment will be a reversal of the creation, and the earth will be left as a chaotic waste and void, as it was in the beginning before God's creative act began (Jer. 4:23-26).

Such destruction, moreover, will come suddenly, like a wall unexpectedly collapsing (Isa. 30:13). So stunning will be the crash that the people will be completely stupified (Isa. 29:9-11). All semblance of order in society will disappear (Isa. 3:1-8; 4:1). The people will be like drunkards, dashed together without any mercy (Jer. 13:12-14). And although their corpses will litter the streets, Yahweh's anger will not be satisfied and his hand will be stretched out still (Isa. 5:25). In that day, we read in Jeremiah (9:21), death will crawl into the windows, and any who remain alive will wish that they were dead (Jer. 8:3). In fact, Amos says that God will literally hunt down his people to slay them, and there will be no hiding place from his destroying anger (Amos 9:1-4).

Israel, the people of the promise, had expected that in the Day of the Lord, that is the day when Yahweh came to manifest his final lordship over the earth, they would be exalted as his chosen nation and their enemies would be destroyed. But the message of the classical prophets is that because Israel has joined the rest of mankind in rebellion against God, they, too, will experience the wrath of the Lord. Indeed, because Israel has enjoyed a special relationship with Yahweh he will experience an especially severe judgment (Amos 2:6-3:2).

> Woe to you who desire the day of the Lord!
>   Why would you have the day of the Lord?
> It is darkness, and not light;
>   as if a man fled from a lion,
>   and a bear met him;
> or went into the house and leaned with his hand
>   against the wall,
>   and a serpent bit him.
> Is not the day of the Lord darkness, and not light,
>   and gloom with no brightness in it?
>
>   (Amos 5:18-20.)

The day of Yahweh's coming will be the time when he will destroy the proud rebellion of his people (Isa. 2:6-21), and his presence with that people will mean the end of them (Amos 8:2). No longer will he have pity on them (Hos. 1:6), no longer will they be his own (Hos. 1:9). The people will seek for Yahweh, but they will not find him, because he will withdraw from them (Hos. 5:6, 15).

> They shall wander from sea to sea,
>   and from north to east;
> they shall run to and fro, to seek the word of the Lord,
>   but they shall not find it.
>
> .   .   .   .
>
>   they shall fall, and never rise again.
>
> (Amos 8:12, 14d.)

Because Israel has forsaken its Lord, Yahweh will forsake Israel (Jer. 7:29). And because Israel has lifted up its voice against him, God will now turn in hatred against his son (Jer. 12:7-8).

What is left of Israel when Yahweh's anger is satisfied will not be worth saving. The people will be like pieces of a broken earthenware pot, not even big enough to use for dipping water (Isa. 30:14; cf. Jer. 19:11). Israel will be as insignificant as two or three berries left at the top of an olive tree after it has been beaten, or like four or five pieces of fruit remaining on a tree that has been stripped (Isa. 17:6). In Amos, that which will remain of the people will be like the fragments of a sheep rescued from a lion by a shepherd—two legs or a piece of an ear (Amos 3:12). The remains will be good for nothing but to be dragged away with hooks to the refuse heap (Amos 4:2-3).

The total prophetic picture which we have of the judgment of God is terrifying in its effect. When we take it seriously, we begin to understand why the New Testament says that "It is a fearful thing to fall into the hands of the living God" (Heb. 10:31). No sincere Christian can read the prophets without a shudder. And having read and understood them, we shall never again be able to take the claims of God's lordship lightly.

There are, to be sure, a few passages in the prophetic writings where it would seem that the fearfulness of this judgment is somewhat mitigated. Sometime during his ministry, Isaiah of Jerusalem issued a fervent call to repentance:

> Come now, let us reason together,
>   says the Lord:
> though your sins are like scarlet,
>   they shall be as white as snow;
> though they are red like crimson,
>   they shall become like wool.
> If you are willing and obedient,
>   you shall eat the good of the land;
> But if you refuse and rebel,
>   you shall be devoured by the sword;
>   for the mouth of the Lord has spoken.
>   (Isa. 1:18-20.)

Amos tells his hearers that if they seek good, they shall live (Amos 5:4, 6, 14), and Jeremiah preaches that if the people amend their ways and their doings and obey the voice of the Lord, the Lord will repent of the evil which he has pronounced against them (Jer. 26:13, 3; 3:11-13; cf. Joel 2:12-13). Yahweh's judgment is not inevitable, and as it is put in Ezekiel, he has no pleasure in the death of the wicked, but desires that the wicked should turn from his way and live (Ezek.

128

18:23; 33:11). There is, however, no compromise here. Israel must renounce its rebellion. The condition of God's salvation is ever surrender to his lordship and complete reliance on him.

When therefore the people reject the call to repentance, when they reply, "We will follow our own plans, and will every one act according to the stubbornness of his evil heart" (Jer. 18:12), Yahweh has no other alternative. He must assert his sovereignty and put down the revolt against him. The people are beyond the reach of all further prophetic guidance, and the prophetic calls to repentance only make them more stubborn and set in their sin (cf. Isa. 6:10). Yahweh's judgment upon them becomes an absolute necessity. "Shall I not punish them for these things," the Lord asks, "and shall I not avenge myself on a nation such as this?" (Jer. 5:9, 29; 9:9.) "How can I pardon you? Your children have forsaken me." (Jer. 5:7.) To try to refine and purify the people further is useless. The wicked are never removed from them. All are but impure metal, which Yahweh has no choice but to reject (Jer. 6:29-30).

The Lord therefore tells the prophet Jeremiah that he is not to make any intercession for the people (Jer. 7:16; 11:14). Even though Moses and Samuel themselves were the intercessors, Yahweh would not listen to them (Jer. 15:1). Nothing can now turn aside the judgment upon God's son. The Lord will consume his people with sword and famine and pestilence (Jer. 14:11-12). Indeed, Jeremiah is not even to enter into mourning for his countrymen, for Yahweh will take away from them every semblance of grace: his peace (shalom), which includes every blessing of life; his covenant love (hesed), which heretofore has always preserved God's relationship with his people; his mercy (rahamim), which has made him pity

129

the people in the past (Jer. 16:5). "What I gave them has passed away from them," Yahweh says (Jer. 8:13). Israel now is completely undone in the sight of his God.

> Surely this iniquity will not be forgiven you
> till you die, says the Lord God of hosts. (Isa. 22:14.)

We must not think, however, that this judgment which Yahweh will execute on Israel is to be carried out with the coldness of an impartial magistrate. Yahweh rises up against his people in the pain and wrath of a disappointed lover. He has offered his people a personal relationship, a relationship of love and trust and faithfulness, but they have completely rejected and rebelled against his love. The One who judges Israel, therefore, is not a cold-blooded executioner, but the husband who has found his wife unfaithful, as we read in Hosea, or the father whose son has turned against him, as it is put in Isaiah and Jeremiah.

The son of the old covenant has been given all and done nothing in return. He has proved himself no longer worthy of his Father's love.

CHAPTER VII

The Prophetic New Israel
And the New Testament Fulfillment
of the Promise

1. THE NATURE OF THE NEW ISRAEL IN THE PROPHETIC WRITINGS

(Read Ezekiel 34-39; Isaiah 40-55)

If judgment is the last word which God's prophets have to speak in Israel's history, then the story of the Old Testament is a meaningless tragedy. It is the story of a unique people destroyed by their lack of faith and their inability to fulfill their destiny in the world. But more than this, if judgment is God's final act in Israel's history, then the Old Testament is a witness to God's weakness and a serious obstacle to the Christian faith. God started something in history, back there in Mesopotamia with Abraham, which he could not finish. He uttered a promise which he could not fulfill. He created a human race over which he could not rule. His lordship was shattered against the unbreachable barrier of Israel's rebellion, and his word was ineffective against the stone shell of Israel's heart. If the last chapter in the story of Israel is that people's destruction, then God has created a world whose evil has overcome him, and our history is subject not to a sovereign Lord but to the rampages of man in successful revolt against his impotent Maker.

The gospel, that is, the good news, of the Bible is the proclamation that God is still in control of his world and that no act of man is able to thwart his completion of his purpose. God promised that through the descendants of Abraham he would restore to all mankind the goodness which he gave them in creation, that Israel would be the means whereby he would bless every nation on the face of the earth, and that Israel's Messiah would be the channel of God's grace to his people. It is the fulfillment of this promise with which the prophets finally deal, and it is in their preaching concerning the new Israel that we find the final witness of the Old Testament to the lordship of Yahweh.

The prophets announce the complete destruction of Israel, but at the same time that they see God destroying his people, they also see him creating a new one. *In one event*, the prophets perceive that God will reject his unfaithful son and bring forth another. *In one act*, the prophets proclaim God will both judge and save. He will not let his promise go unfulfilled, for he will create a new Israel, and by means of this new people he will bring blessings on all mankind.

This new Israel will have a continuity with the old. He will be of the seed of Abraham and share in the Davidic promise. Yet in his relationship to God the new Israel will differ radically from the past. He will be everything that the community of the old covenant was meant to be, do everything that the chosen people from the first were elected to do. The new

Israel, in short, will fulfill the old Israel's obedience. He will perfectly manifest the lordship of Yahweh in his life.

The basis for the new Israel's obedience will be Yahweh's transformation of his inner life, and the Lord will create this new people by giving them a new heart and spirit.

A new heart I will give you, and a new spirit I will put within you; and I will take out of your flesh the heart of stone and give you a heart of flesh. And I will put my spirit within you, and cause you to walk in my statutes and be careful to observe my ordinances. (Ezek. 36:26-27; cf. 11:19.)

The result is that Israel will now be able to enter into an intimate and personal relationship with his Lord. Gone will be the spirit of harlotry (Ezek. 37:23; 36:25; Isa. 4:4) and the desire for rebellion (Isa. 43:25-44:5; 44:22-23). The people will now have a new heart to know Yahweh as the ruler of their life (Jer. 24:7). His commandments for them will no longer be external laws, but desires consonant with the leanings of their own hearts, and no one will need to teach another that Yahweh is Lord, because all will know him as Ruler, from the least to the greatest among the people (Jer. 31:33-34; cf. Isa. 11:9).

Yahweh, then, will be able to enter into a new marriage with Israel, his wife. Now he can heap his compassion and love upon her (Isa. 54:1-8; 49:13-26). Now he can woo her again and lead her out into the desert, and there betroth her to himself in righteousness and mercy and faithfulness (Hos. 2:14-17, 19-20). Or to change the figure, now Yahweh can reclaim his son (Isa. 49:14-16), his servant whom he has created for himself. Now he can have pity on him who was not pitied (Hos. 2:23). Now he can establish with him an everlasting relationship (Isa. 54:9-10; Ezek. 37:26-27; 34:30-31; 16:60, et al.). In fact, so close will be Israel with his God that all will be the recipients of Yahweh's spirit, prophesying in his name (Joel 2:28-29).

The dominant characteristic of this new Israel in this new relationship with Yahweh will be Israel's complete trust and reliance on the Lord. This will once again be a holy people (Isa. 4:3), separated and responsible to God alone. They will no longer follow the directions of their own will, but they will accept Yahweh's instructions (Isa. 29:24), wholeheartedly giving the guidance of their life over to him (Jer. 24:7). Like lame men, they will depend completely upon Yahweh for their power to walk (Mic. 4:5-7), and he will show them the paths to follow. In fact, Yahweh himself will be their shepherd (Ezek. 34:11-16). He will feed them in good pasture, and gather the lambs in his arms, and carry them in his bosom, and gently lead those that are with young (Isa. 40:11). And the people will follow him, humbly and faithfully (Zeph. 3:11-13). The Lord will be their sole support and their place of refuge (Isa. 4:6; 14:32). They will trust in him forever (Isa. 26:1-6), and therefore none shall make them afraid (Zeph. 2:13). "They shall sit every man under his vine and under his fig tree" (Mic. 4:4), in an eternal realm of peace (Isa. 2:4), and all nature will combine together to bless and prosper their life (Isa. 11:6-9; Ezek. 34:25-31). The new Israel will be a people of faith, living in obedient intimacy with the Lord, and therefore their life will reflect all of the full goodness of God's original creation (Isa. 51:3; Ezek. 36:35).

This new people of God, however, will not live for themselves alone. Rather, God can now use them for the purpose for which Israel was first created. Now the new Israel can be the channel of God's blessing on all mankind. Because the new Israel will be a people of faith, Yahweh will make them the cornerstone of the new Zion (Isa. 28:16). That is, Jerusalem and its temple here are thought of as incarnate, and God will no longer be worshiped in a temple made of stone. Now he will be revealed and present in a living congregation. Now he will be made known through the new Zion, the people of faith (Isa. 51:16; 52:8). Because God has created this new people, his work in them will be the revelation of himself throughout the earth (Isa. 52:10), a memorial and an everlasting sign of the Lord which shall not be cut off (Isa. 55:13). Just as the glory of the Lord descended to the temple of Solomon (I Kings 8:11), so now his glory will be seen in his creation of the new Israel, the incarnate temple (Isa. 44:23; 46:13; 49:3; 40:5). And the new Israel will become his witness, the revelation of Yahweh, to the ends of the earth (Isa. 43:10, 12; 44:8; 55:4). The people of faith, the incarnate Zion, will become Yahweh's herald of good tidings (Isa. 40:9; 41:27). The new Israel will be the center from which Yahweh's word will go out through all the world (Isa. 2:2-3; Mic. 4:1-2).

This incarnate Zion will form the core, then, of a new, universal congregation of peoples. No longer will nation compete and war against nation (Isa. 2:4; Mic. 4:3), but now all nationalism will be overcome, and all peoples on the face of the earth will become the people of Abraham (Ps. 47:9-10). All nations will serve God as members of his church, and Assyria and Egypt and Israel will all worship the Lord together (Isa. 19:23-25; cf. Ps. 82:8). In short, the promise to Abraham in Gen. 12:3 will be fully and finally fulfilled. Through the new people of Abraham, the people of faith, the incarnate

Zion, all nations will find their revelation of God and their spiritual home.

These same thoughts are expressed in another way in the prophecies of Second Isaiah (Isa. 40-55). Here the new Israel is not only the incarnate Zion. He is also the incarnate covenant. He is Yahweh's servant, whom the Lord has given to be a covenant to all of the nations of the earth:

> I am the Lord, I have called you in righteousness,
> I have taken you by the hand and kept you;
> I have given you as a covenant to the people,
> a light to the nations.

> (Isa. 42:6; cf. 49:8.)

That is, the new Israel is the means whereby Yahweh enters into relationship with all other peoples (cf. Isa. 52:13-53:12). Now there is no formal ceremony on Mount Sinai, no pact made between God and the nations of the earth. Now the new Israel is the guarantee that God is not only with one people, but with all peoples, and the work which God does on behalf of the new Israel is done for the benefit of all.

As this incarnate covenant, the new Israel is, again, the center of revelation. It is through the new people of God that Yahweh's covenant law is made known to all peoples (Isa. 42:4; 51:4). Now God guides not only one people by means of his law. Now he guides all of the peoples on earth. All are drawn into the congregation of the chosen people. Through the incarnate covenant, the new Israel, all are blessed with God's favor.

We have seen previously that the king in Israel was the embodiment or personification of the people's life (see Chapter V). So, too, in the new age, the king or Messiah will embody all these characteristics of the new Israel in his person. In fulfillment of God's promise to David, the Messiah will be a shoot from the stump of Jesse (Isa. 11:1). He will come from the city of Bethlehem in Judah, from which sprang the Davidic house (Mic. 5:2; cf. I Sam. 17:12), and he will occupy the throne of King David (Isa. 9:7; Jer. 23:5; Ezek. 34:23-24; 37:24-25). Because all peoples will be members of one congregation, this Messiah will rule over a universal kingdom (Mic. 5:4; Zech. 9:10; Isa. 55:3-5). But like the new Israel in its relationship to God, the Messiah will act by inner dependence on the Lord. No longer will his rule be a matter of military or political strategy. Now it will be grounded on the Messiah's relation to God. It is because the Messiah will be given the spirit of the Lord (Isa. 11:2) that he will be able to reign in justice and righteousness and faithfulness (Isa. 11:4-5; Jer. 23:6; Isa. 42:1). It is because Yahweh will give him strength that he will be able to lead his people (Mic. 5:4). He will not be a military conqueror, but a man of peace, humble and riding on an ass, the beast of peaceful pursuits:

> Rejoice greatly, O daughter of Zion!
>   Shout aloud, O daughter of Jerusalem!
> Lo, your king comes to you;
>   triumphant and victorious is he,
> humble and riding on an ass,
>   on a colt the foal of an ass.
> I will cut off the chariot from Ephraim
>   and the war horse from Jerusalem;
> and the battle bow shall be cut off,
>   and he shall command peace to the nations;
> his dominion shall be from sea to sea,
>   and from the River to the ends of the earth.
>   (Zech. 9:9-10.)

137

This Messiah will reign over a kingdom in which no one shall hurt or destroy (Isa. 11:9; 9:7) and in which no good thing will be lacking (Ezek. 34:25-31). And through this perfect king, God will bestow on all peoples his goodness (Isa. 55:1-5, 12-13). Through the new Israel and its Messiah, God will fulfill his promise.

2. JESUS CHRIST, THE NEW ISRAEL, THE FULFILLMENT OF THE PROMISE

The crucial question of biblical faith is, Did it ever take place? Did God actually keep his word? Did he destroy the people of the old covenant, as the prophets had proclaimed he would do? Did he in reality create a new Israel and inaugurate the messianic reign? Or were the prophets merely visionaries, preaching sermons unrelated to history? Is the Old Testament story a fairy tale having no basis in fact?

To ask the question of the historicity of the Bible is to inquire after the foundations of our faith. For if God's judgment and new creation never actually took place, then the prophets' words, for all of their poetry, are completely irrelevant, the idle musings of religious dreamers having no relationship to our life. If, however, these prophetic words came to pass, then sometime in our history, the kingdom of God has begun to break into time and space, and there has been reintroduced the goodness of God's creation. More, God has kept his promise and has triumphed over the evil rebellion of man. History is subject to his lordship, and he cannot be defeated. The whole structure of our faith depends on whether or not God has fulfilled his word. To ask, "Did it ever take place?" is ultimately to ask if there is anything to believe at all.

It has long been the view that the prophetic proclamations

of judgment and of salvation came to pass in the exile and return of the Hebrew people in the eighth, sixth, and fifth centuries B.C. Certainly this view is not without foundation. It cannot be doubted that the prophets themselves saw the exile as a judgment of God upon his sinful people, and certainly when the northern kingdom of Israel fell to Assyria in 721 B.C., the ten tribes of the north were completely destroyed, or at least lost, in history. Such an event would seem the confirmation of the words of Amos or Hosea, just as the Babylonian exile of 587 B.C. seems a fulfillment of the preaching of the prophets in the south. Again, the prophets themselves see God's merciful hand in the return of the Babylonian exiles to Palestine, and the restoration of the postexilic congregation would seem the fulfillment of their preaching concerning the new Israel.

Nevertheless, it is questionable if the events of the exile and return *exhaust* the content of the prophetic proclamations of judgment and salvation. Certainly the Babylonian exile, at least, did not destroy the old Israel. Those who remained alive and who returned from exile considered that they made up the kingdom of God on earth (Ezek. 43-48; cf. I Chron. 28:5; 29:23; II Chron. 13:8). For a time, it was considered that Zerubbabel, the governor of Judah from the line of David, would be appointed as messianic ruler over this congregation (Hag. 2:21-23), and that this remnant of the old Israel would be exalted at the expense of its enemies (Ezek. 38-39).

One can, however, find little evidence that the postexilic community was a new, or even a purified, people. The postexilic prophets such as Trito-Isaiah (Isa. 56-66) and Haggai and Malachi found much in the post-exilic Israel to remind them of the rebellion of the old Israel, and one searches in vain in the Old Testament for any evidence that the restored Judean community became the center of a universal congregation of God. In fact, just the opposite took place, and the legalism which followed the work of Nehemiah and Ezra tended to separate and distinguish the Jews from the surrounding peoples. If we must view the return from exile and the restoration as the fulfillment of the prophetic proclamations of salvation, then it must be admitted that it was a bleak fulfillment at best, and that the prophets engaged in a good deal of wishful hyperbole. We may admire Second Isaiah's rapturous hymns of promise and his heart-warming pleas to his people to "wait upon the Lord" and thereby to become the Servant through whom God could redeem all people (Isa. 52:13-53:12), but we must admit that the postexilic congregation never really fulfilled the prophet's words.

We have, in truth, perhaps laid too much emphasis on the events of the exile and return in our interpretations of the Old Testament. For startling as it may seem, the New Testament not once includes the Babylonian captivity or the return from Babylon in the account of God's acts in history. The word "exile" is never used in the New Testament, and Babylon is mentioned only in the genealogy of Matthew 1, in a quotation from Amos in Acts 7:43, and as a symbol of evil in the Revelation of John. The New Testament follows the course of the Old from the patriarchs up through the Judges, David, and the monarchy, and then it stops. Nothing more is made of Israel's history after the monarchy, and the exile is not considered to be an integral part of God's saving history.

The New Testament does, however, know a judgment against men in which all of the evil and rebellion of mankind against God are done away. This judgment centers in the person of Jesus Christ, and more specifically in his death and resurrection. The whole story of the Passion of our Lord clearly betrays his rejection at the hands of his own people, and the New Testament makes clear that he is also suffering the judgment of God. Paul affirms that the whole curse of Israel's disobedience, centering on its disregard of the law, has fallen upon Christ (Gal. 3:13), and therefore Christ suffers the fate which inevitably attends such sin against God (cf. II Cor. 5:21). Christ dies the death which is the reward of rebellion against God (Rom. 6:23).

His death, however, is not an isolated event. All of mankind participates in that death, and thus all of mankind has been subjected to the judgment of God. Paul states this in unmistakable terms: "We are convinced that one has died for all; therefore all have died" (II Cor. 5:14).

No man can escape this judgment, because all men have taken part in the rebellion against God (cf. Rom. 3:10-19). Therefore, when Christ dies upon the cross, all of mankind suffers judgment. When Christ is buried, rebellious mankind is buried with him. In these events, the judgment which was announced by the prophets is effected. With the death of Jesus, Israel dies too. They exist no more as the people of the Lord. All that Israel is, is totally and finally rejected by God. Israel nails God's Son to the cross, and in that act brings destruction upon itself (John 3:19).

At the same time, however, the New Testament sees in the death and more particularly in the resurrection of Christ, God's creation of the new Israel, and thus of a new mankind. If all men participate in the judgment of God when Christ dies, then it is equally clear that all men will benefit from God's vindication of Christ when he raises him from the dead

141

(Rom. 5:18-19). With the resurrection of Jesus, a new creation is begun (II Cor. 5:17), because that Resurrection means that the judgment of God has been fulfilled, and the results of man's rebellion have been overcome (Col. 2:13-14). If Israel is rejected in the death of Jesus, they are created anew in his resurrection. This is the significance of the fact that in the book of Revelation, the twelve gates of the city wall, named for the twelve tribes of Israel, stand upon twelve foundations, named for the twelve apostles of Jesus (Rev. 21:12-14). Israel is restored and renewed when God's new covenant community, the church, results from the resurrection of our Lord.

The New Testament authors affirm and reaffirm this fact. For example, Jesus is understood as the incarnate Zion, as the temple in Jerusalem made flesh. Jesus himself uses this figure when he speaks of raising a destroyed temple in three days (John 2:19; Matt. 26:61; 27:40). As Jesus has replaced the temple, so also the chief activity centered in the temple, the worship of God, has been transferred to him. Jesus refers to this fact when he tells the Samaritan woman that the former places of worship, Mt. Gerizim (the mountain of the Samaritan temple in the north), and Jerusalem in the south, have been supplanted. Jesus has now become the way to the Father (John 14:6; cf. Acts 4:12; Rom. 5:1). This fact lies behind John's vision of the New Jerusalem: "And I saw no temple in the city, for its temple is the Lord God the Almighty and the Lamb" (Rev. 21:22). Zion has now become the place of the Lamb, and of his redeemed (Rev. 14:1).

As the incarnate Zion, Christ becomes, as in the Old Testament prophecies, the core of a universal congregation of believers. In I Pet. 2:4 ff., he is the cornerstone mentioned in Isa. 28:16, which the Lord has laid in Zion, the beginning of "a chosen race, a royal priesthood, a holy nation, God's own people." That is, Christ is the foundation stone of God's new Israel, and in him, the beginning of a new people is made. Similarly, in Eph. 2:18-22, Christ is the chief cornerstone of the temple of God into which all faithful believers are built. He is the beginning, the core, of the new people of faith. In him, the promises of the prophets find fulfillment.

It is not surprising, then, that John 1:14 says that in this word made flesh, this incarnate fulfillment of the Old Testament proclamation, we beheld the glory of God. For we must remember that it was to the temple, and earlier the tabernacle, that the glory of God descended. And Christ as the incarnate temple reflects this same glory, just as does the new Israel in the prophecies of Second Isaiah.

So, too, Jesus is the incarnate covenant, the guarantee that God is with all men (Eph. 2:12-18). Through the cup of the New Covenant in his blood (I Cor. 11:25; Mark 14:24; Matt. 26:28), mankind's sins are forgiven (Heb. 10:11-18). His death on the cross becomes the basis of our peace with the Father.

> he was wounded for our transgressions,
>   he was bruised for our iniquities;
> upon him was the chastisement that made us whole,
>   and with his stripes we are healed.
>
> (Isa. 53:5.)

That which God wrought in Jesus Christ is done on behalf of us all, and Jesus is the mediator of our relationship with God (Heb. 8:6; 12:24).

Through every book of the New Testament this fulfillment

in Christ can be traced. He is the new Israel and the new Messiah, upon whom the spirit of God is poured out. He is the descendant of David, ruling over a universal kingdom. He is the Messiah of peace, bringing justice and righteousness and faithfulness to his people in the strength of the Lord. In infinite detail, the New Testament proclaims that this was the One expected. On page after page, it testifies that God has kept his promise.

Perhaps first and foremost, however, we should understand Jesus Christ as the fulfillment of Israel's obedience. The people of the old covenant were called to serve the Lord as his son. God brought them out of Egypt into a good land, flowiug with milk and honey. He gave them a law to govern their life and fought before them in their battles. He set a king to reign over them, and raised up prophets to guide them. He asked only in return that they love him and trust him and let him rule their hearts and wills. He asked of this son surrender, in order that the son might be the instrument of God's redemption of the world. But Israel could not trust the Lord or walk in his commandments. Israel was a rebellious son, hardhearted and unloving.

God therefore replaced Israel with a new and faithful Son, a Son who in every respect was tempted like Israel, and like we are, yet without sinning (Heb. 4:15). Through the course of the Gospel stories we can trace his obedience: his refusal in his desert temptations to serve any other ruler but God (Matt. 4:1-11), his rejection of even the closest human ties as more important than his relationship with his heavenly Father (Matt. 12:46-50), his total subjection of man's life with man to God's will and purpose for the community (Matt. 5-7), his constant refusal in his dealings with the scribes and

Pharisees to conform to merely human standards of morality and religion. In every deed and word, Jesus acknowledged the sole lordship of God, until his obedience brought him finally to a dark garden called Gethsemane, where in sorrow and agony, he sweated out his final surrender, "Father, if thou art willing, remove this cup from me; nevertheless not my will, but thine, be done" (Luke 22:42).

Here was the true Son of God. Here was the descendant of Abraham and of David who perfectly followed his heavenly Father. Here was the new Israel, the one of unshakeable faith. Here was the obedient Israel whom God could use for his purpose. Jesus Christ was everything that God had intended Israel to be, everything for which Israel had been created in the beginning. In him and him alone, God's lordship was perfectly made manifest. In him and only him, God's rule was clearly seen, God's kingdom was come on earth, even as it is in heaven. Jesus Christ perfectly exercized the obedience which Israel owed to its Lord. He was the one true and faithful Son of God.

The rest of us, both within and without the Christian church must realize, however, that Jesus Christ is also the fulfillment of the obedience which we owe to the Father. We are in nature little different from Israel, from God's people in the Old Testament. Like Israel in the wilderness, we have been redeemed by an act of God and given a new life of which we are completely unworthy: "While we were yet sinners Christ died for us" (Rom. 5:8). Christ has died on a cross for the whole lot of us, no matter to which segment of mankind we belong. Those of us within the church have further entered into covenant with God. In receiving the sacraments of the

145

church, we have promised to serve God as the Lord of every realm of our life.

Yet, every man, within or without the church, stands worthy of the judgment of his Maker. Indeed, those of us who belong to the church are especially guilty before God. For having been given his word and spirit to guide us, we have often stubbornly refused to follow either. We can claim no special piety which exempts us from God's wrath. Far from letting God order the community of the church in peace and love and justice, we have torn it with the strife of dispute and hatred and gossip. Far from being the center from which God's word goes out into the world, we have been a confusion of tongues, veiling God's revelation with the deceit of our own opinions. Far from being the core of a universal congregation, we have barred the poor, the colored, the outcast from finding a spiritual home in our sanctuaries.

We therefore stand guilty before God, and he declares to us as he declared to Israel, "What right has my beloved in my house, when she has done vile deeds?" (Jer. 11:15). We Christians have no right in God's house, because of the things we have done. Because of our refusal to let God be our Lord, our prayers, like Israel's, weary God's soul, and our worship to him is an odious hypocrisy. Judged on the basis of our works alone, we are deserving of nothing other than the destruction which befell Israel, and we can expect no more than the rejection and desolation meted out to the original people of Yahweh. The judgment, announced by the prophets, is the wages of our sin against God. The Christian church has earned no more than its own destruction from its Lord.

In short, we Christians are joined together with the rest of mankind, as was Israel, in a common rebellion against God.

Like Eve in the garden of Eden, or all nations at the tower of Babel, all of us, both in and without the church, have tried to get along without God. It is not his commandments and rule we have honored, but our own wisdom and self-will. It is not God's power upon which we have waited, but the armed might and decisions of men. It is not the Lord's glory we have sought, but the rewards of human fame and fortune. And all of us, from the least to the greatest, now stand culpable before God. We are deserving of the manifestation of his lordship in his judgment upon us.

Only one person stands between us and the wrath of the Lord—Jesus Christ, the only obedient Son of God. In him, we are judged, to be sure. In his death on the cross God fully and finally rejects all that we are and claim to be. When Jesus dies on Golgotha, all mankind is killed with him. Not one of us, the Cross tells us, can expect any other than death. But it is the message of Easter morn that death is not God's last word toward the obedience of Jesus Christ, and he is shown in his resurrection to be acceptable to God. This one Man, obedient and faithful even to the Cross, is raised up and received into the household of his Father. Jesus Christ alone can enter into life with God. He only is deserving of all of God's blessing.

We however can participate in the resurrection of Christ. We can be recipients of the eternal life and goodness given to him. We can be received into the household of God, counted as true and obedient sons of our heavenly Father. Through faith in Jesus Christ, through clinging to him—in moments both of certainty and those of deepest doubt, in times of nobility and those of darkest deeds, crying out, "Lord, I believe, help thou my unbelief"—through letting Christ hold

147

on to us, though the devil himself would wrench us free, we can share in Christ's obedience before the Lord. By holding fast to Jesus Christ, we participate in his life. We become members of his very body. God counts his obedience and faithfulness as ours, and we become parts of him, the new Israel.

In Christ, then, we are delivered from God's final judgment. We are raised out of death and given eternal life. We are restored to the communion and goodness of God. In Christ, our odious worship is made acceptable to the Father. In Christ's name, our prayers are heard by the Lord. As members of Christ's body, we belong in God's house. Through faith in him, we are counted as belonging to God's people. Jesus Christ alone fulfills our obedience. In him only is our rebellion overcome.

God kept his promise to the fathers. He raised up a faithful Son, a descendant of Abraham and of David, through whom he blessed all peoples on the face of the earth. We need only accept in faith this blessing which has been given. This is God's answer to man's revolt. This is the final sign of his lordship, that our sin is unable to overcome God's purpose for his world, that despite all that we have done against him, God has kept his word. Nothing has been able to deter God from fulfilling his promise. Nothing can overcome this Lord of our history.

Who, then, is Jesus Christ? He is the fulfillment of the Old Testament story. He is the new Israel, God's faithful and obedient Son. He is the guarantee that God controls our history. He is our way to life, to goodness, and to blessing. He is the promise of God made flesh and come to pass for the redemption of the world.

AIDS TO FURTHER BIBLE STUDY

Bright, John. *A History of Israel.* 2nd. ed. Philadelphia: Westminster Press, 1972.

———. *The Kingdom of God.* Nashville: Abingdon Press, 1953.

Kelly, Balmer H., ed. *The Layman's Bible Commentary.* 25 vols. Richmond: John Knox Press, 1959–64.

Krodel, Gerhard, ed. *Proclamation Commentaries: The New Testament Witnesses for Preaching.* Philadelphia: Fortress Press, 1975–.

McCurley, Foster R., ed. *Proclamation Commentaries: The Old Testament Witnesses for Preaching.* 7 vols. Philadelphia: Fortress Press, 1977–79.

Sandmel, Samuel et al., ed. *The New English Bible with the Apocrypha: Oxford Study Edition.* New York: Oxford Univ. Press, Inc., 1976.

Tucker, Gene M., ed. *Guides to Biblical Scholarship: Old Testament Series.* Philadelphia: Fortress Press, 1971–.

Via, Dan O., Jr., ed. *Guides to Biblical Scholarship: New Testament Series.* Philadelphia: Fortress Press, 1969–.

Westermann, Claus. *Handbook to the New Testament.* Minneapolis: Augsburg Publishing House, 1969.

———. *Handbook to the Old Testament.* Translated by Robert H. Boyd. Minneapolis: Augsburg Publishing House, 1967.

Wright, George E. and Filson, Floyd V. *The Westminster Historical Atlas to the Bible.* Rev. ed. Philadelphia: Westminster Press, 1956.

For the Advanced Reader . . .

Eichrodt, Walther. *Theology of the Old Testament.* 2 vols. Translated by J. Baker. Philadelphia: Westminster Press, 1967.

von Rad, Gerhard. *Old Testament Theology.* 2 vols. New York: Harper & Row, 1962 & 1965.

INDEX OF SCRIPTURAL REFERENCES

151